# COLOURSUTRA

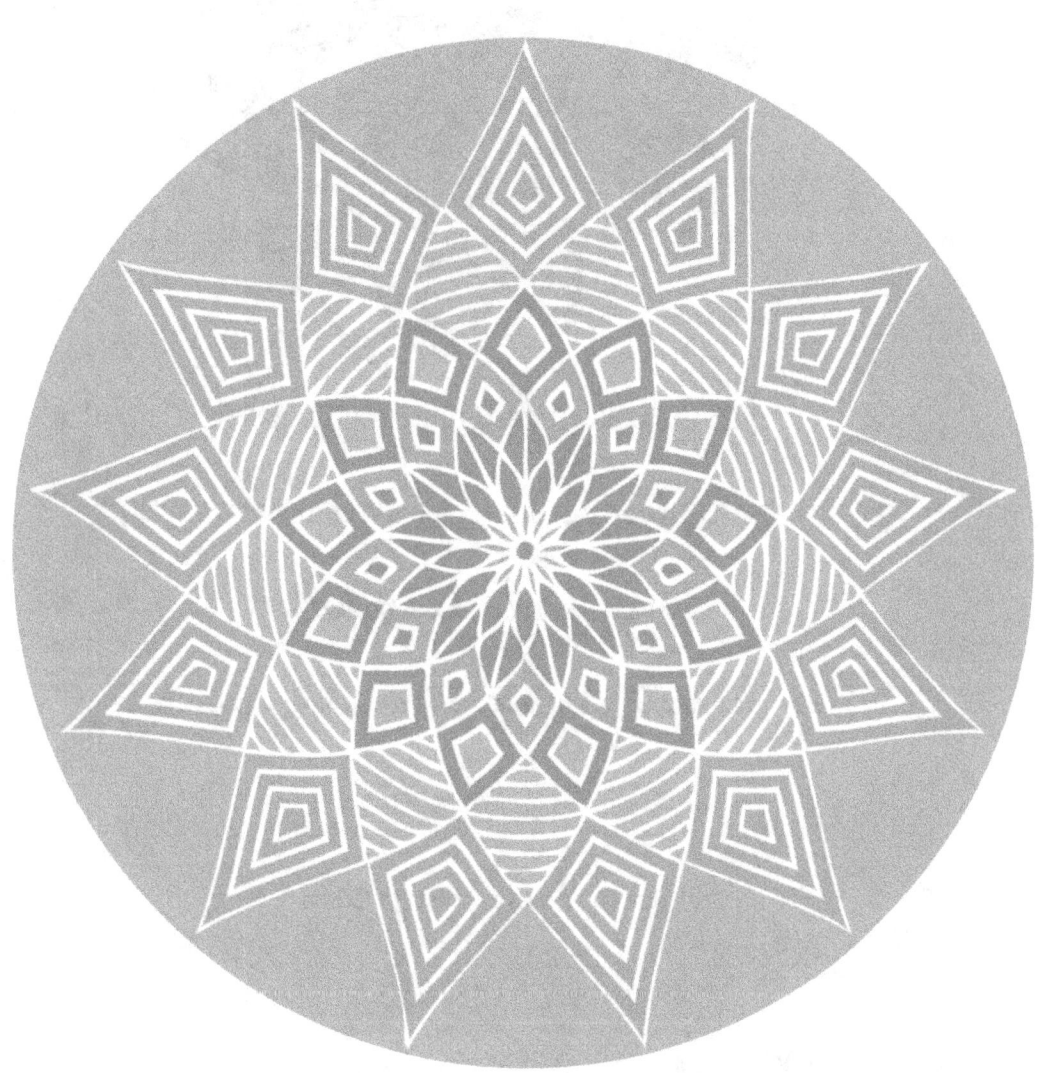

# Colouring Book For Adults
## The Ultimate Stress Reliever

Created by Sofy Rahman

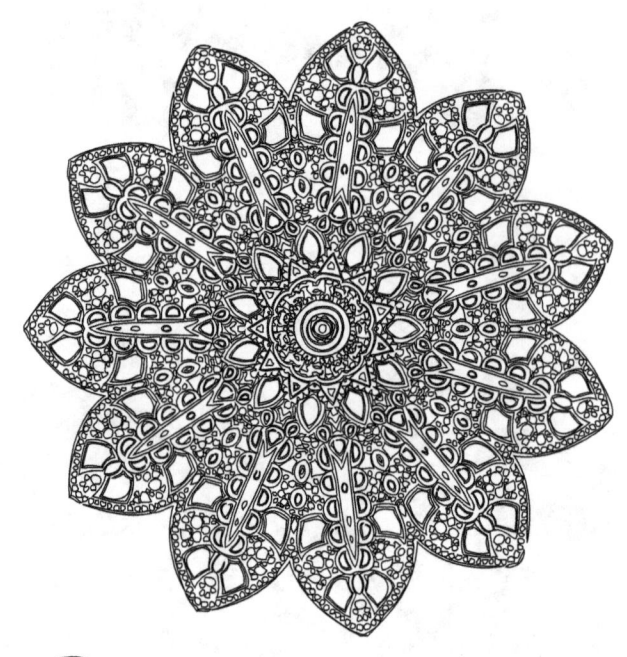

Specially dedicate this book
to both sets of my late grandparents,
my lovely husband,
my dearest parents and mum in law,
my family
and lastly my cats.


May this colouring book brings joy
to you and brings out the child
in every single one of you.

Happy Colouring!

# Introduction

Have you always wanted to find a way to destress? If so, you are not alone.

Colour therapy is one of the most popular methods of relaxation at the moment.

Couple that with some soothing music, and you will find that it can be extremely enriching.

When was the last time you actually held a colour pencil, and let it flow

 across a clean white page?

Growing up, I was introduced to the joy of art classes at the tender age of 5.

Oh the joy of colouring and drawing with oil pastels, coloured pencils and other

medium!

Honestly , I lost touch with my creative side when I was at the peak of my youth as other

distractions and interests entered my life.

 As I got older, experiences I gained from frequent travelling, further inspired me

to reconnect with my creative self, propelling me to produce the designs in this book.

No one can deny the therapeutic effect colouring can have on one's well being;

in fact it can even soothe  the savage beast!

I found that colour therapy really helped me in more ways than one.

Apart from the many colouring books available out there, why not challenge yourself to

this book?

It offers a 50-day challenge to complete all 50 designs.

As simple as that!

When we put our minds into completing a page a day,

we not only  destress ourselves and improve our colouring,

but we also exercise - it disciplines us.

So , are you ready to take up this 50 day challenge with me?

Come join me and the rest of the Coloursutra community on Facebook today!

**https://www.facebook.com/groups/coloursutra/**

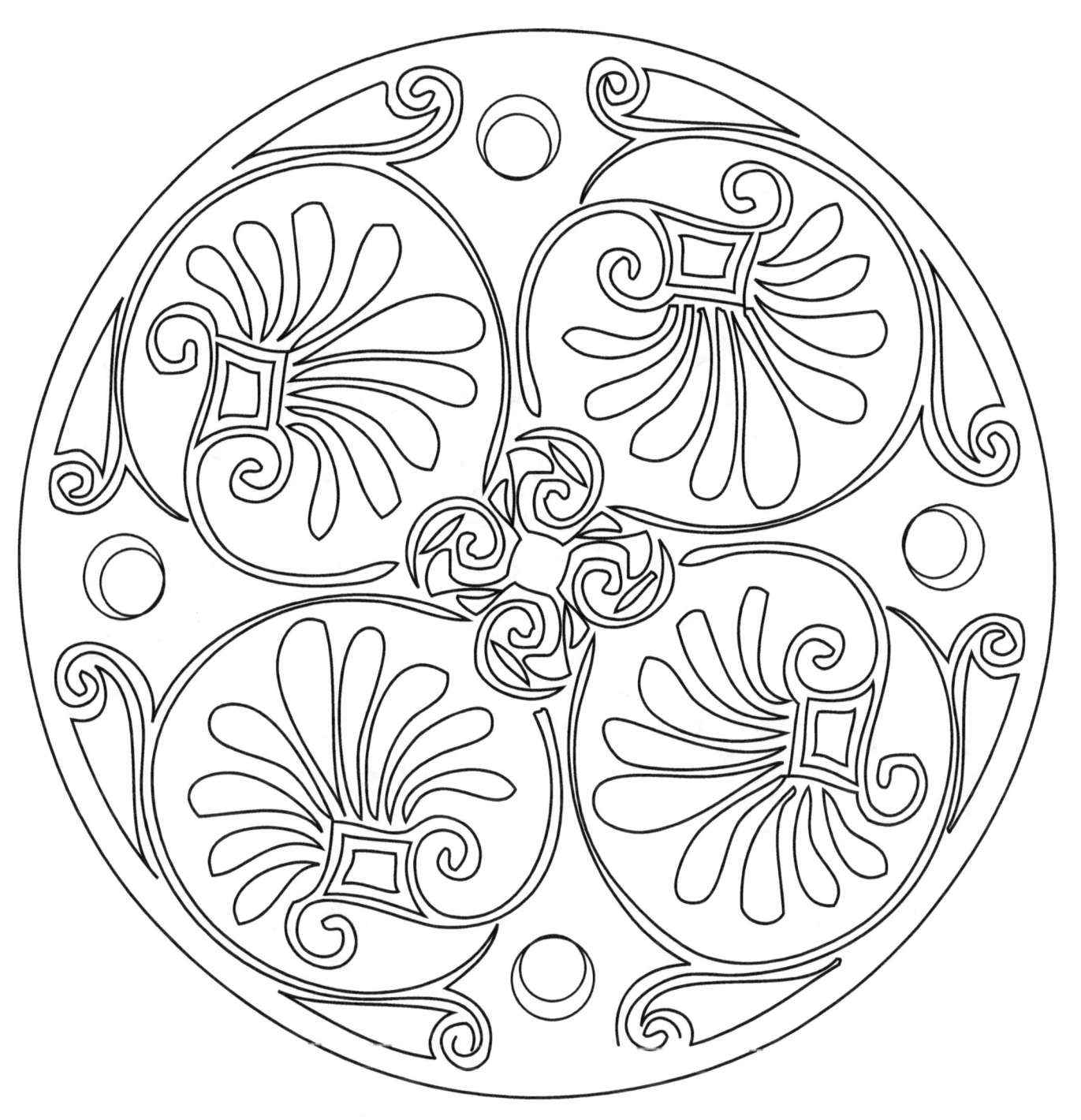

THINK OF ALL THE BEAUTY LEFT
AROUND YOU AND BE HAPPY
- ANNE FRANK

IT'S THE FIRE THAT BURNS...
BUT IT ALSO LIGHTS THE WAY.
- BETH SAWICKIE

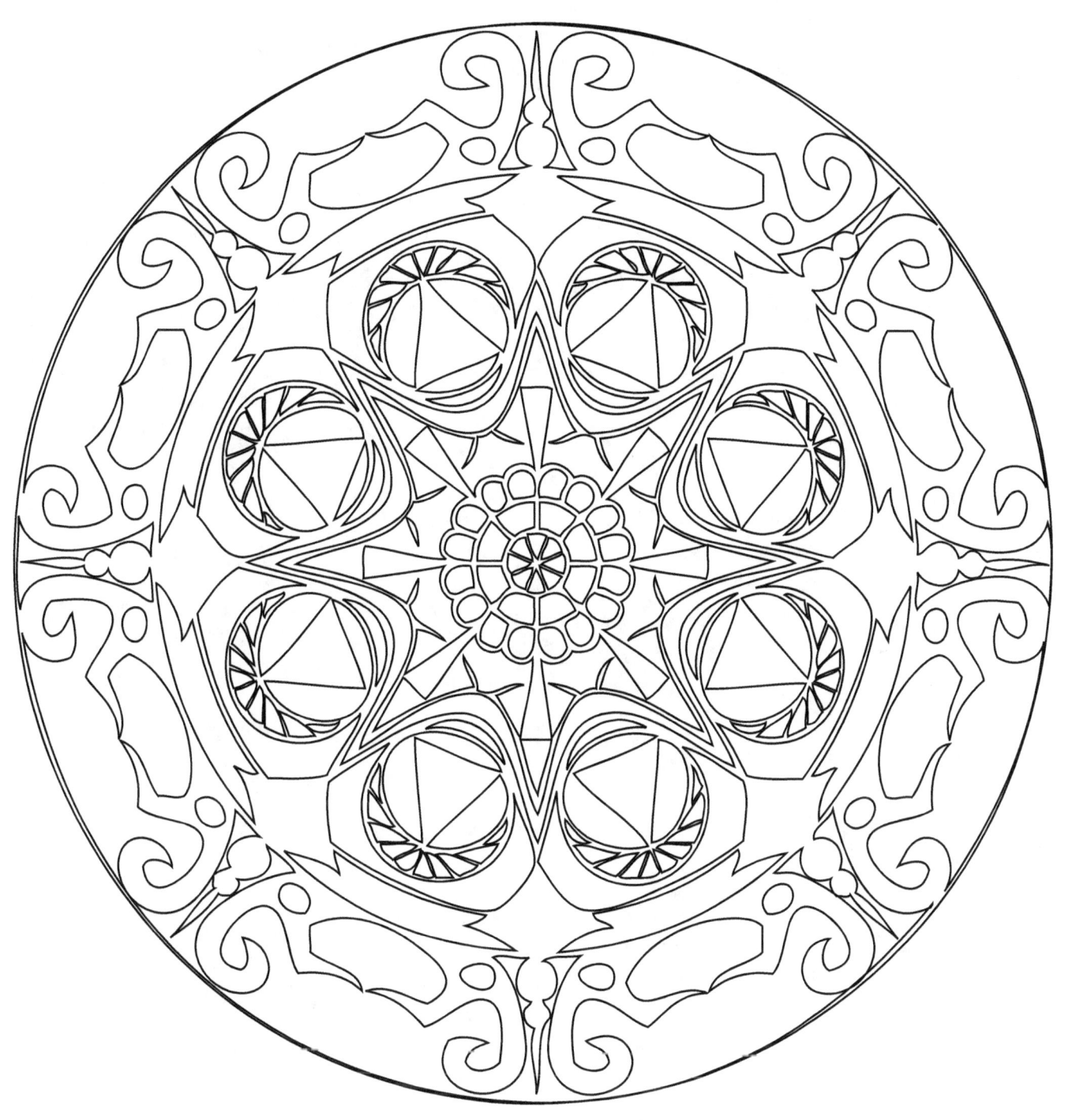

YOU MUST BE THE CHANGE YOU WISH
TO SEE IN THE WORLD.
- GANDHI

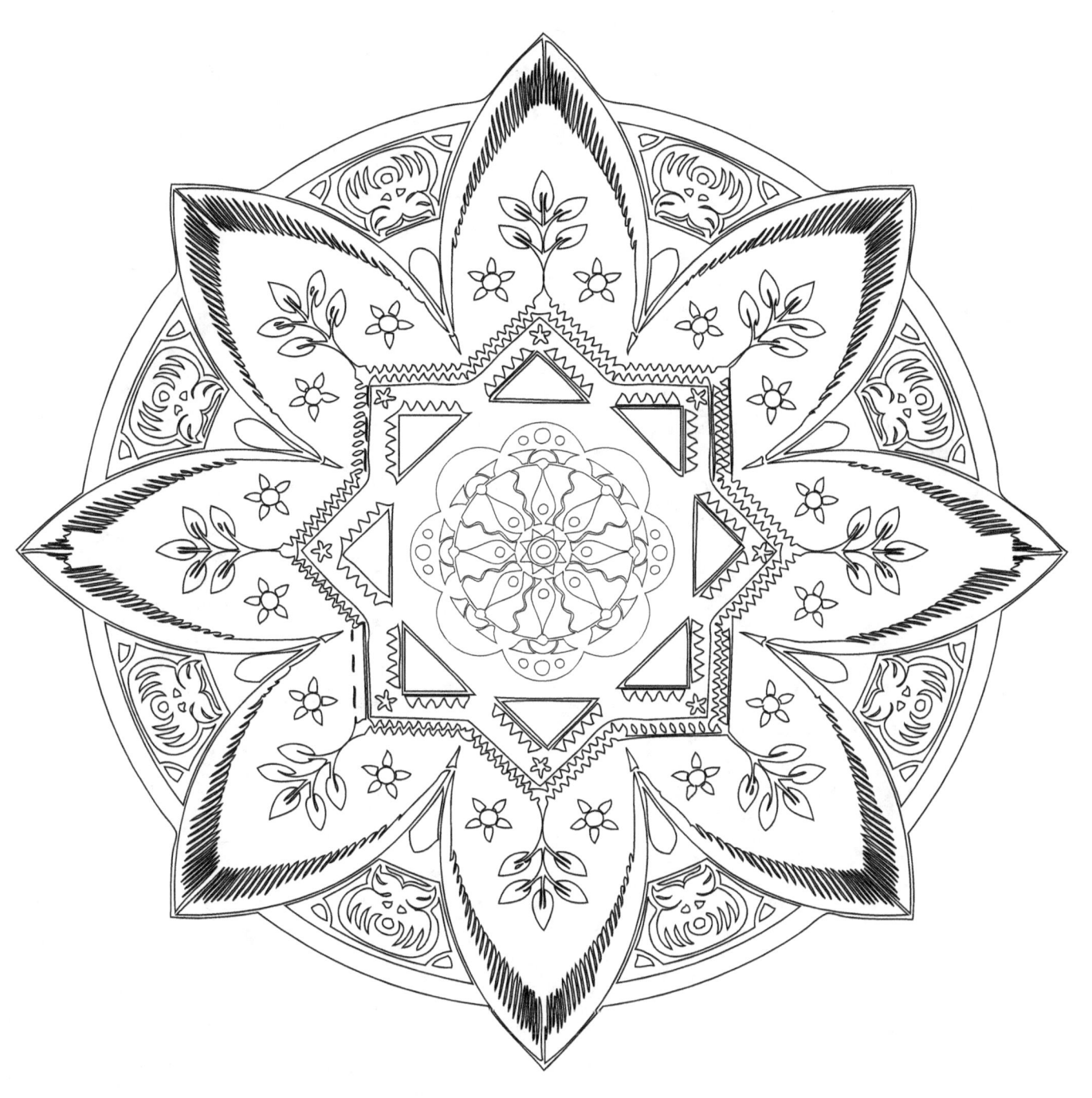

LOVE MELTS THE HARDENED HEART,
SO TURN UP THE HEAT.
- AARON CONN

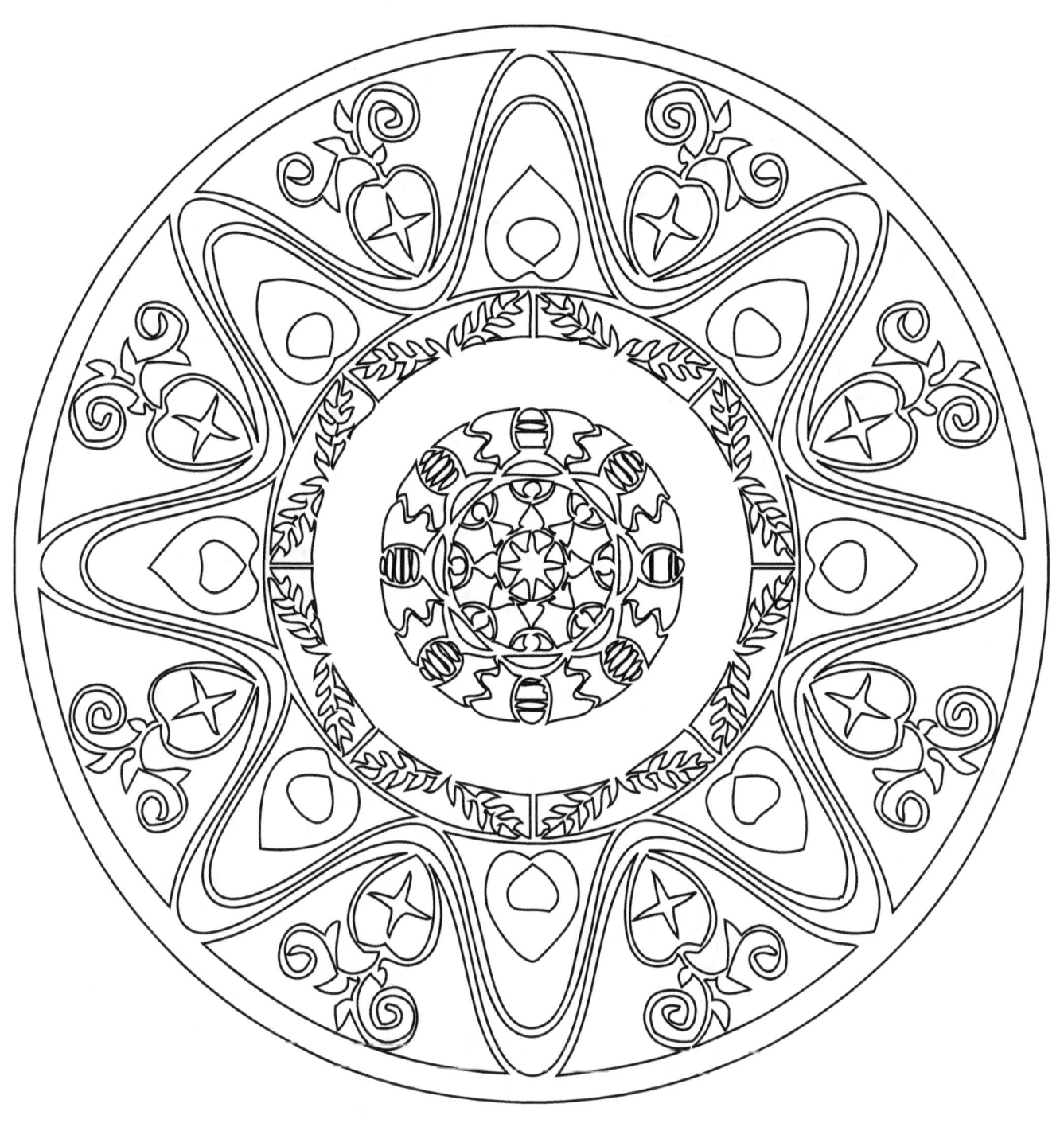

EVERY CHILD IS AN ARTIST, THE PROBLEM
IS STAYING AN ARTIST WHEN YOU GROW UP.
- PABLO PICASSO

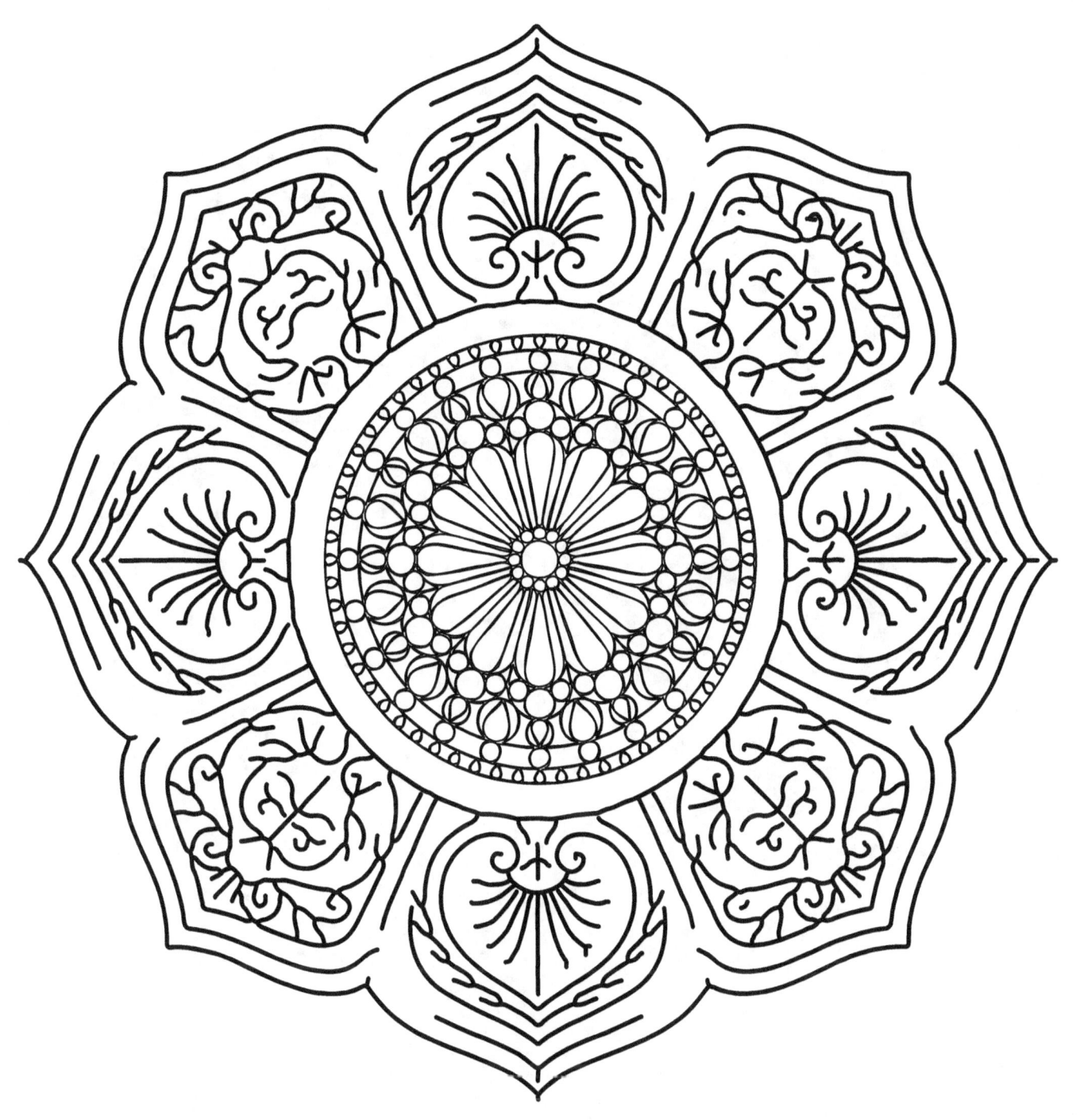

ALL THAT WE ARE IS THE RESULT OF WHAT WE
HAVE THOUGHT. THE MIND IS EVERYTHING
WHAT WE THINK WE BECOME.
- BUDDHA

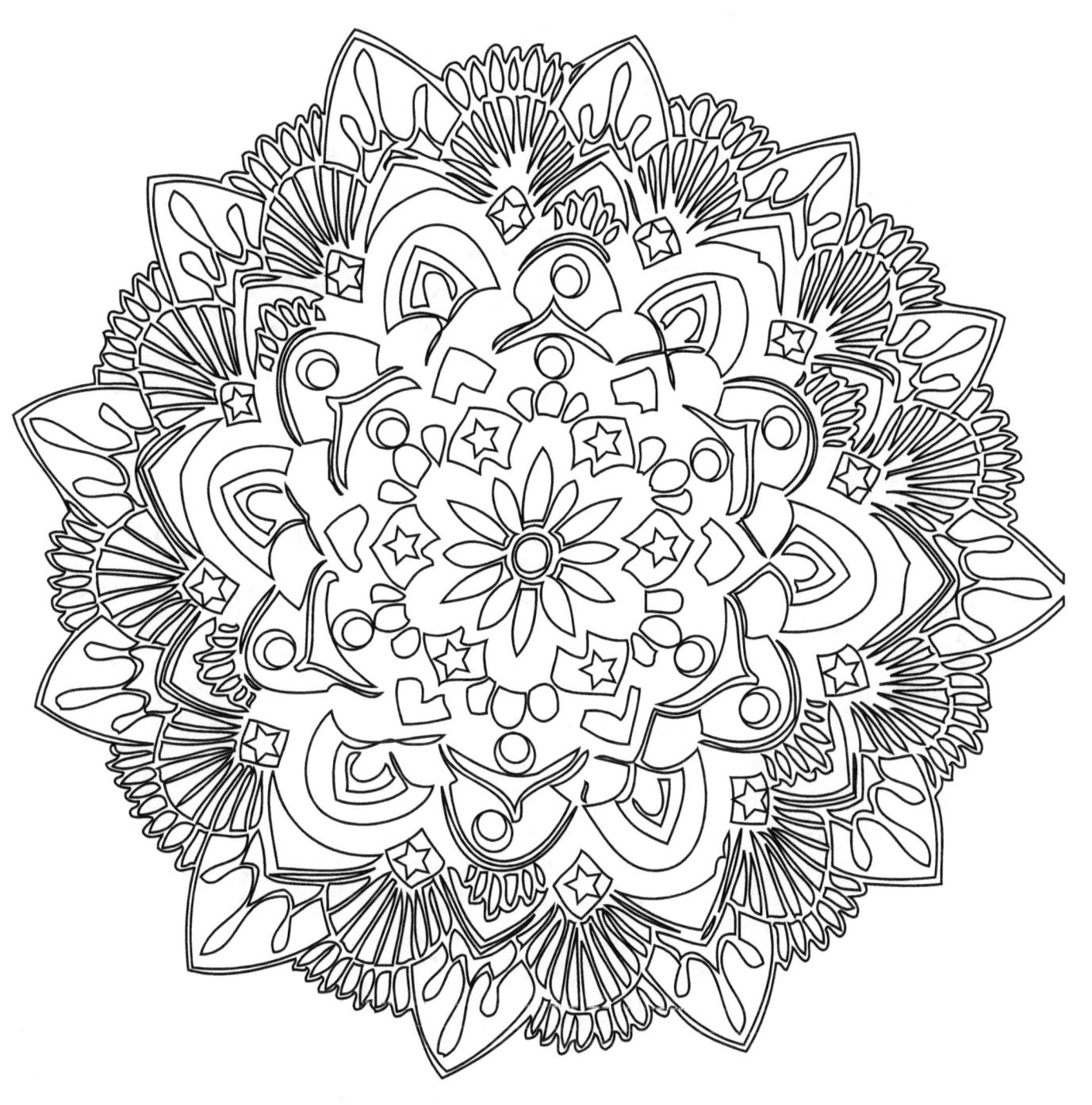

DON'T TELL PEOPLE YOUR DREAMS.
SHOW THEM.

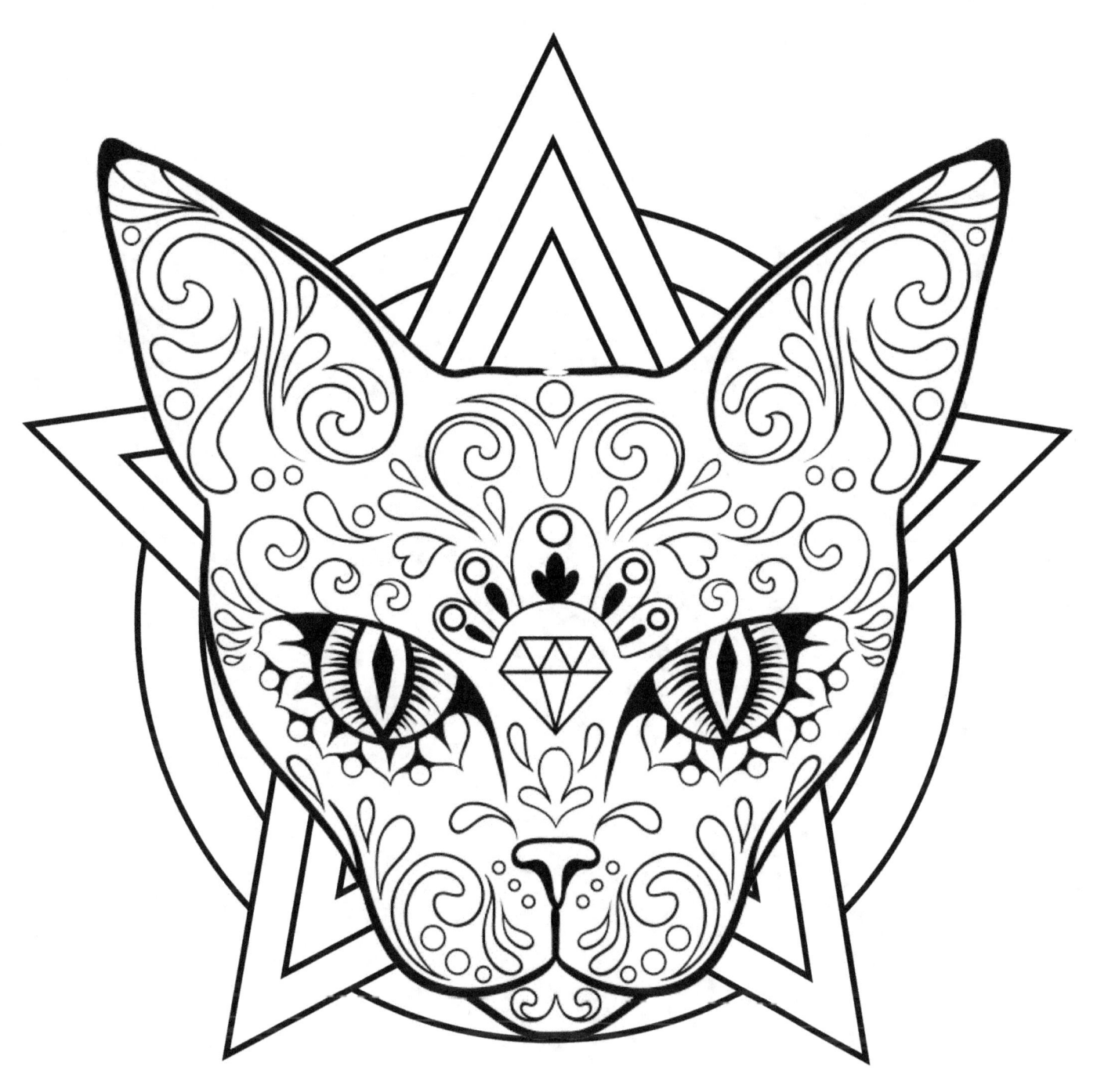

DO NOT LET *WHAT YOU* CANNOT DO
INTERFERE *WITH WHAT YOU* CAN DO.
- JOHN *WOODEN*

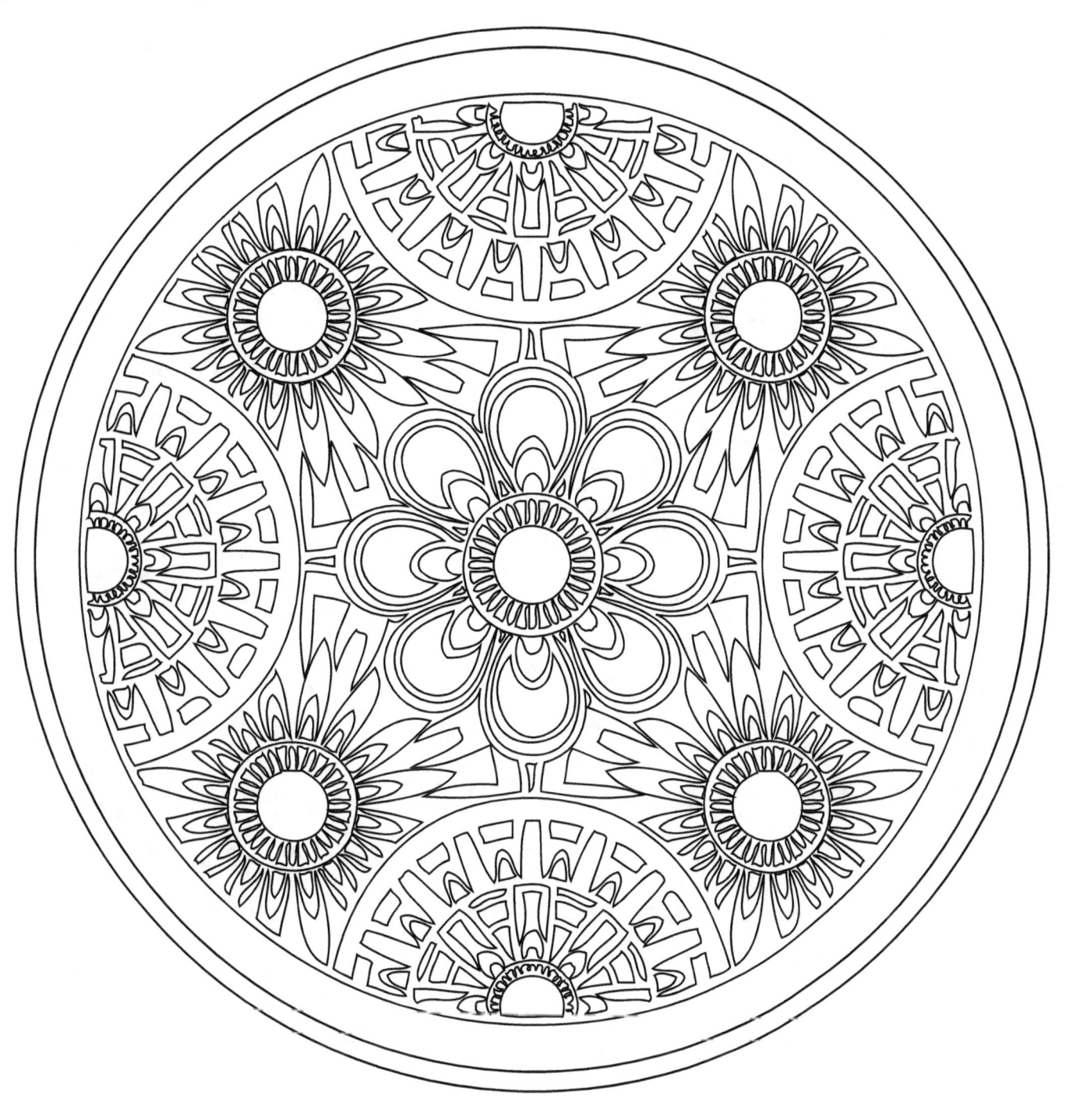

LIVE EACH DAY AS IF YOUR LIFE
HAD JUST BEGUN.
- JOHANN WOLFGANG VON GOETHE

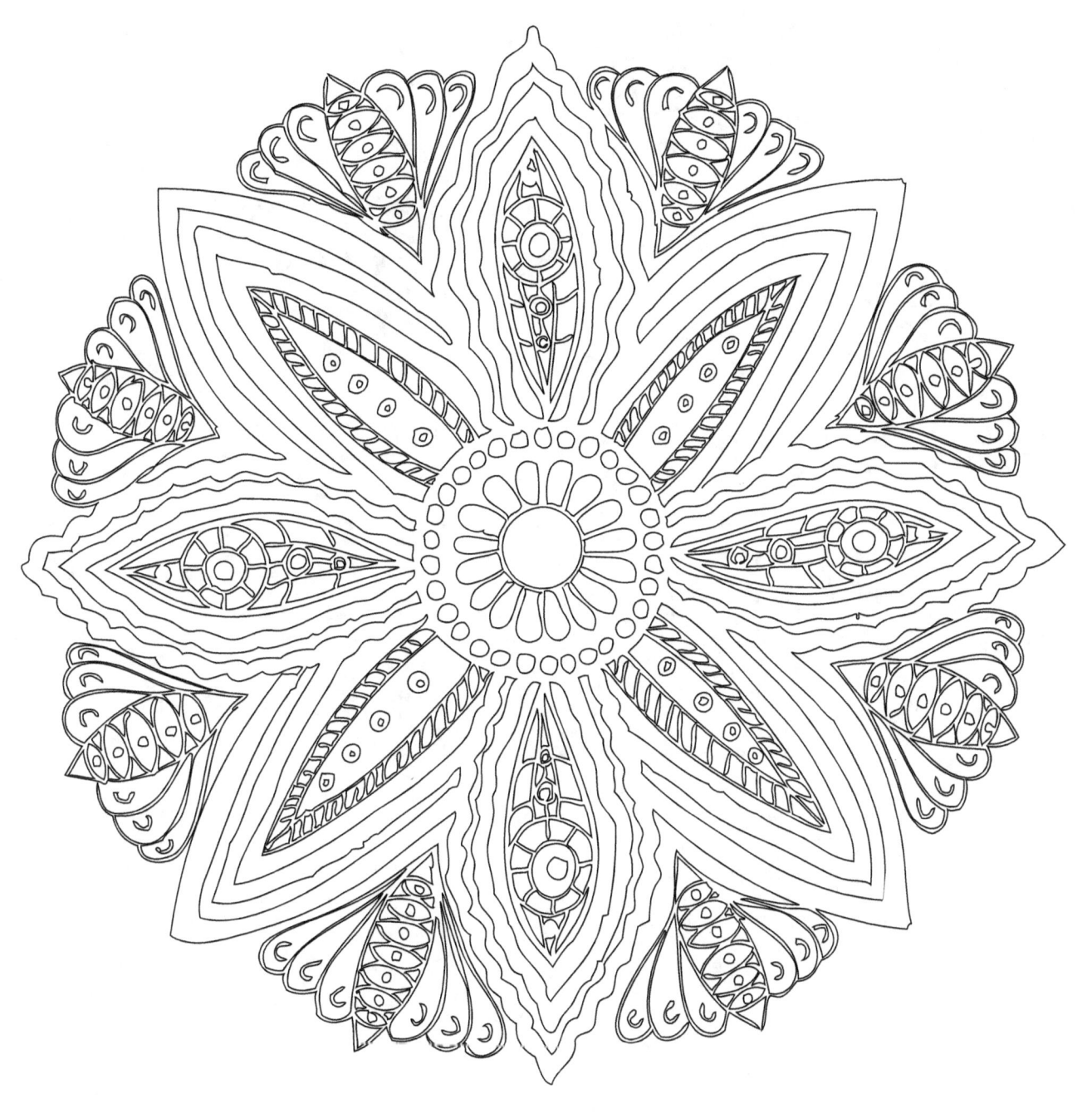

BE NOT AFRAID OF LIFE. BELIEVE THAT
LIFE IS WORTH LIVING,
AND YOUR BELIEF WILL HELP CREATE THE FACT.
- WILLIAM JAMES

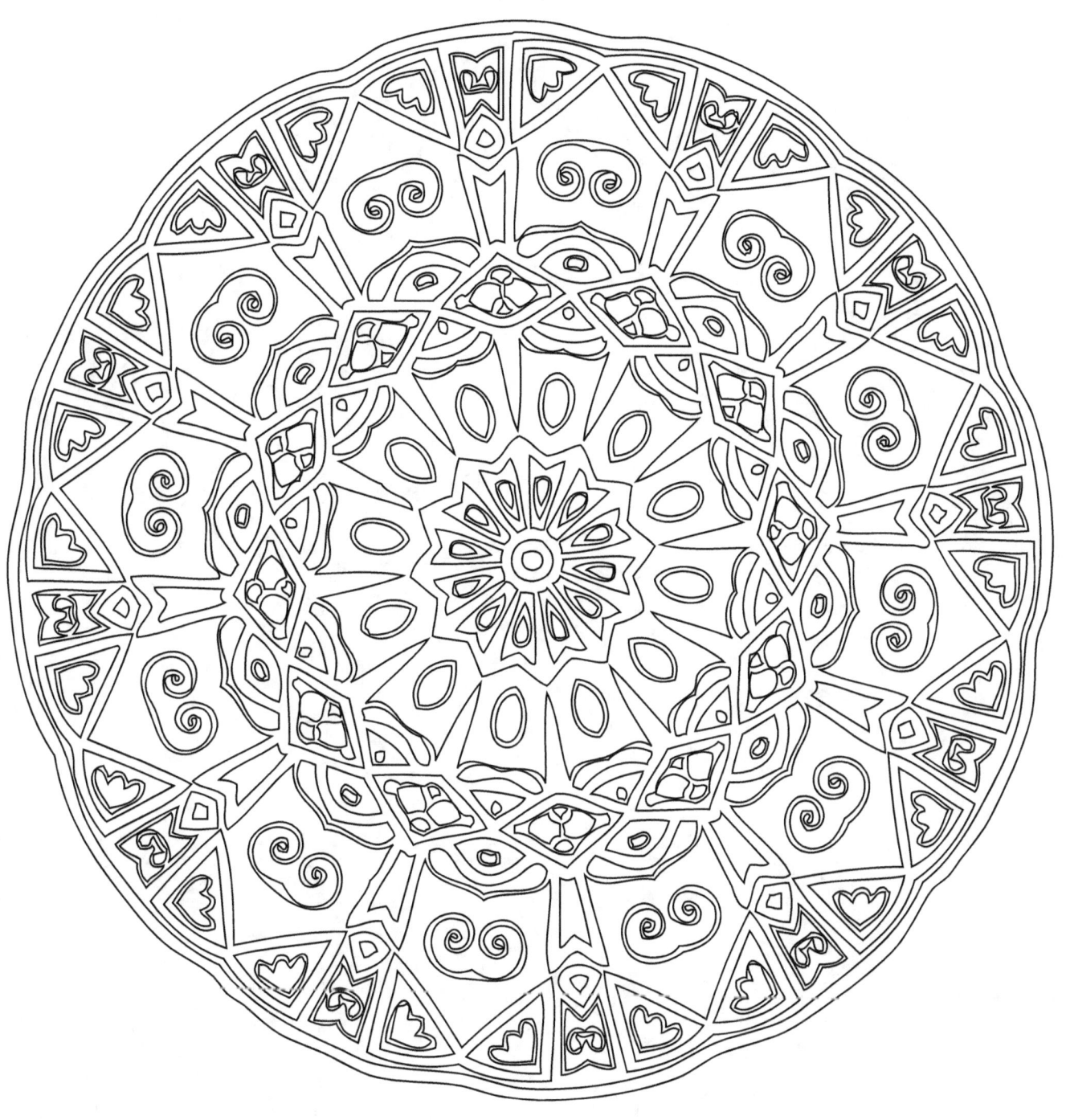

THE REAL OPPORTUNITY FOR SUCCESS LIES
WITHIN THE PERSON AND NOT IN THE JOB.
- ZIG ZAGLER

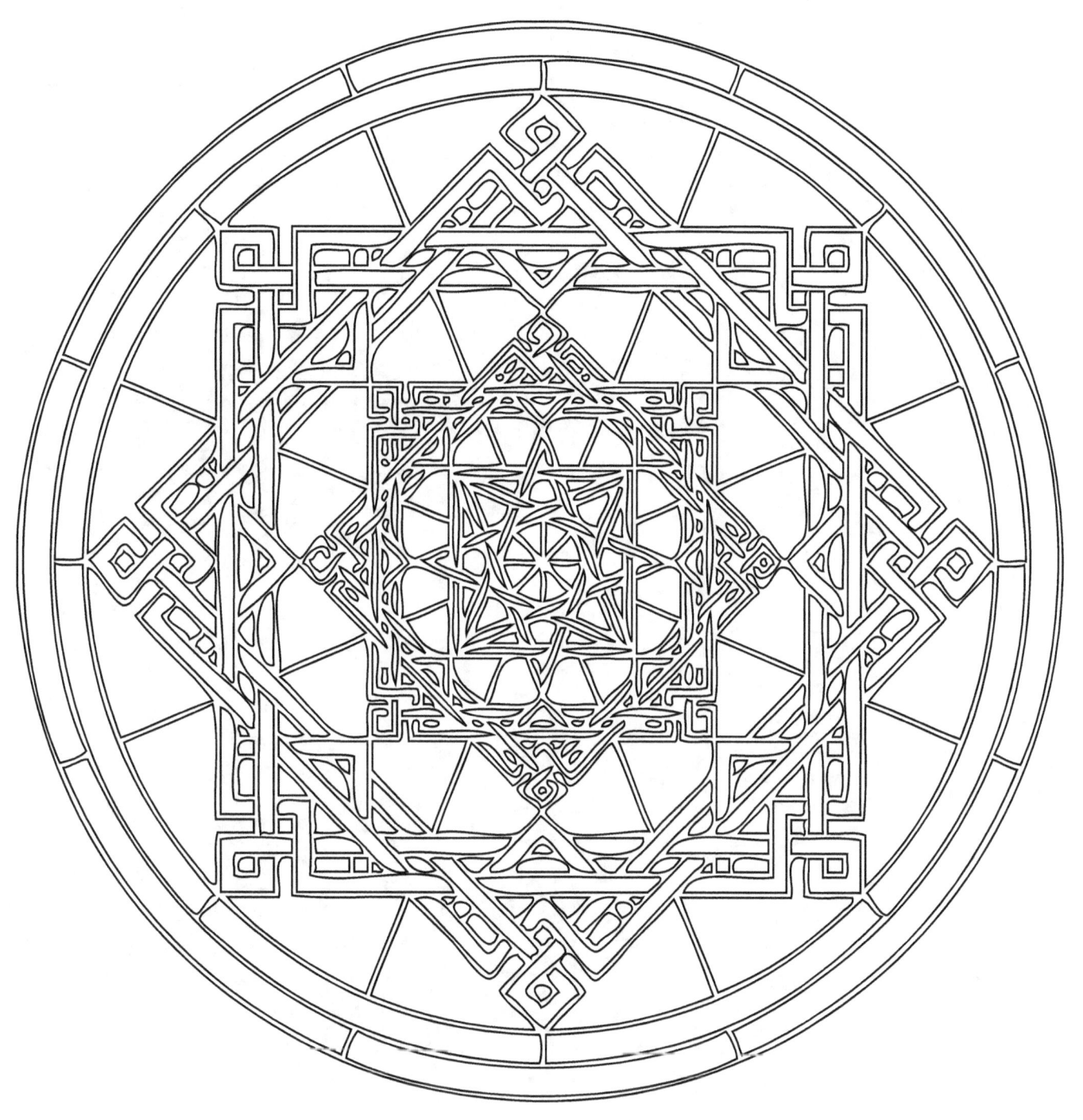

WHOEVER LOVES MUCH, PERFORMS MUCH,
AND CAN ACCOMPLISH MUCH,
AND WHAT IS DONE IN LOVE IS DONE WELL
- VINCENT VAN GOGH

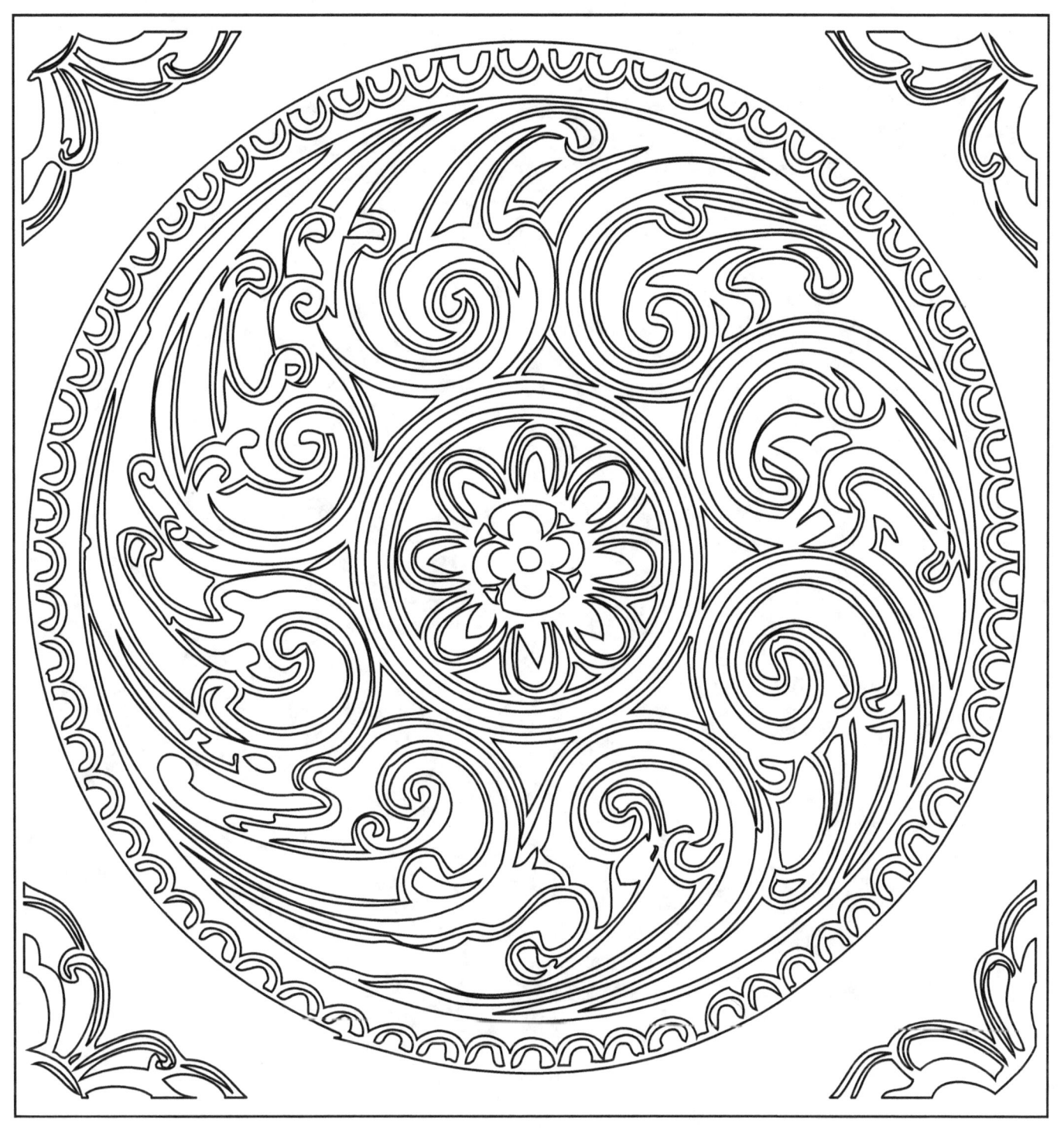

LIVE EACH DAY AS IF YOUR
LIFE HAD JUST BEGUN.
- JOHANN WOLFGANG VON GOETHE

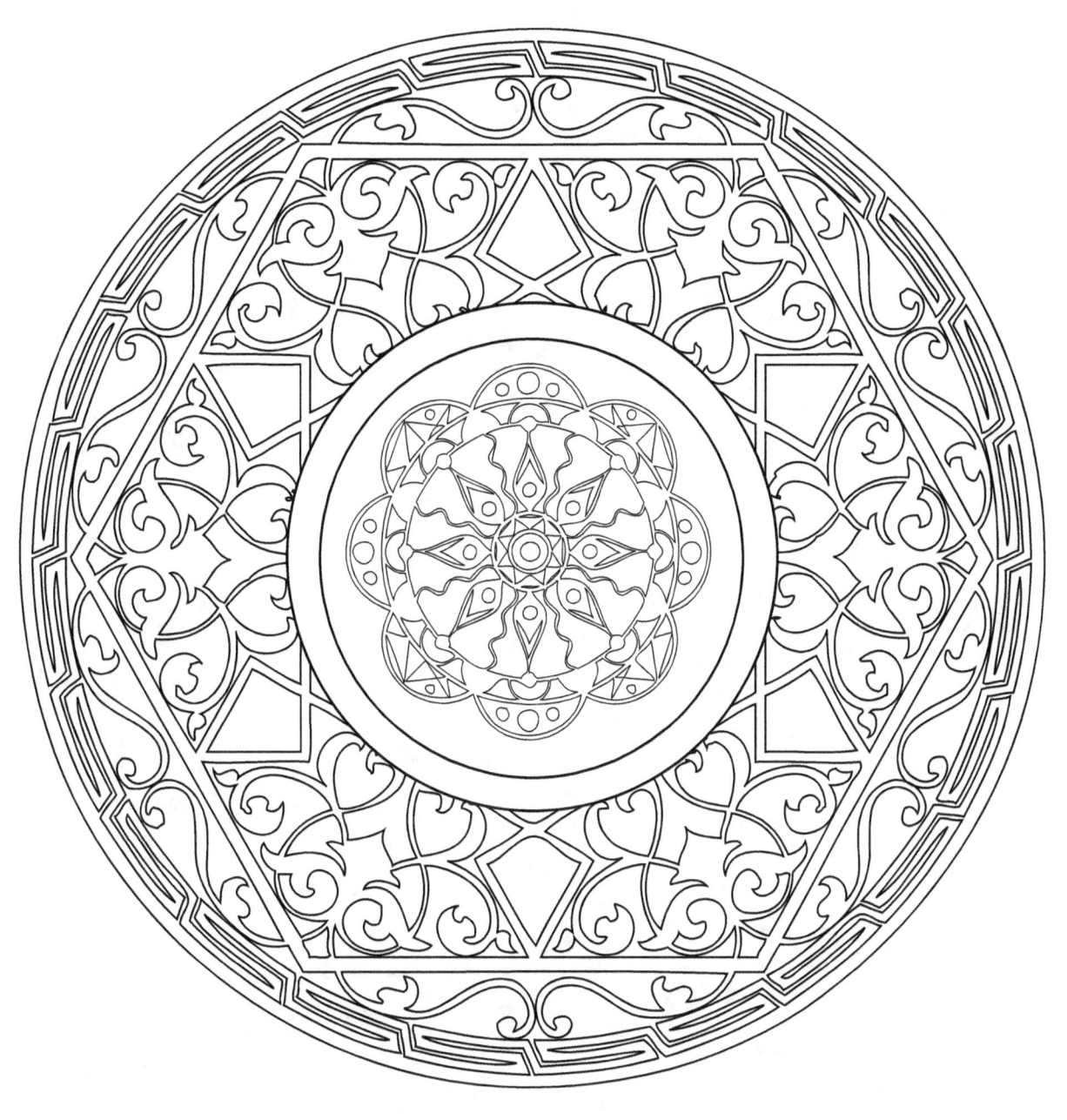

DON'T WORRY ABOUT FAILURES, WORRY ABOUT
THE CHANCES YOU MISS
WHEN YOU DON'T EVEN TRY.
- JACK CANFIELD

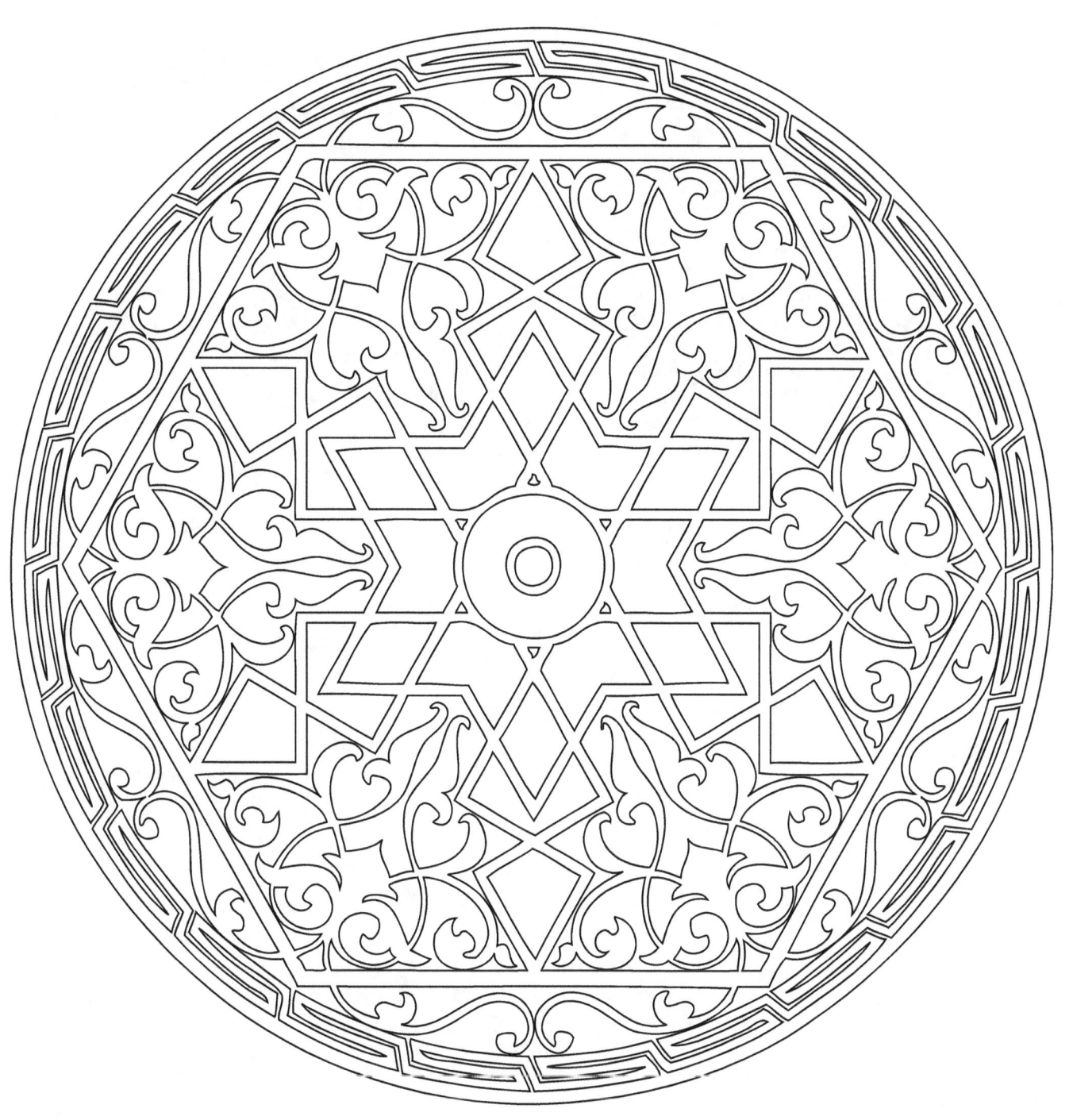

I DON'T KNOW THE KEY TO SUCCESS,
BUT THE KEY TO FAILURE IS
TRYING TO PLEASE EVERYBODY.
- BILL COSBY

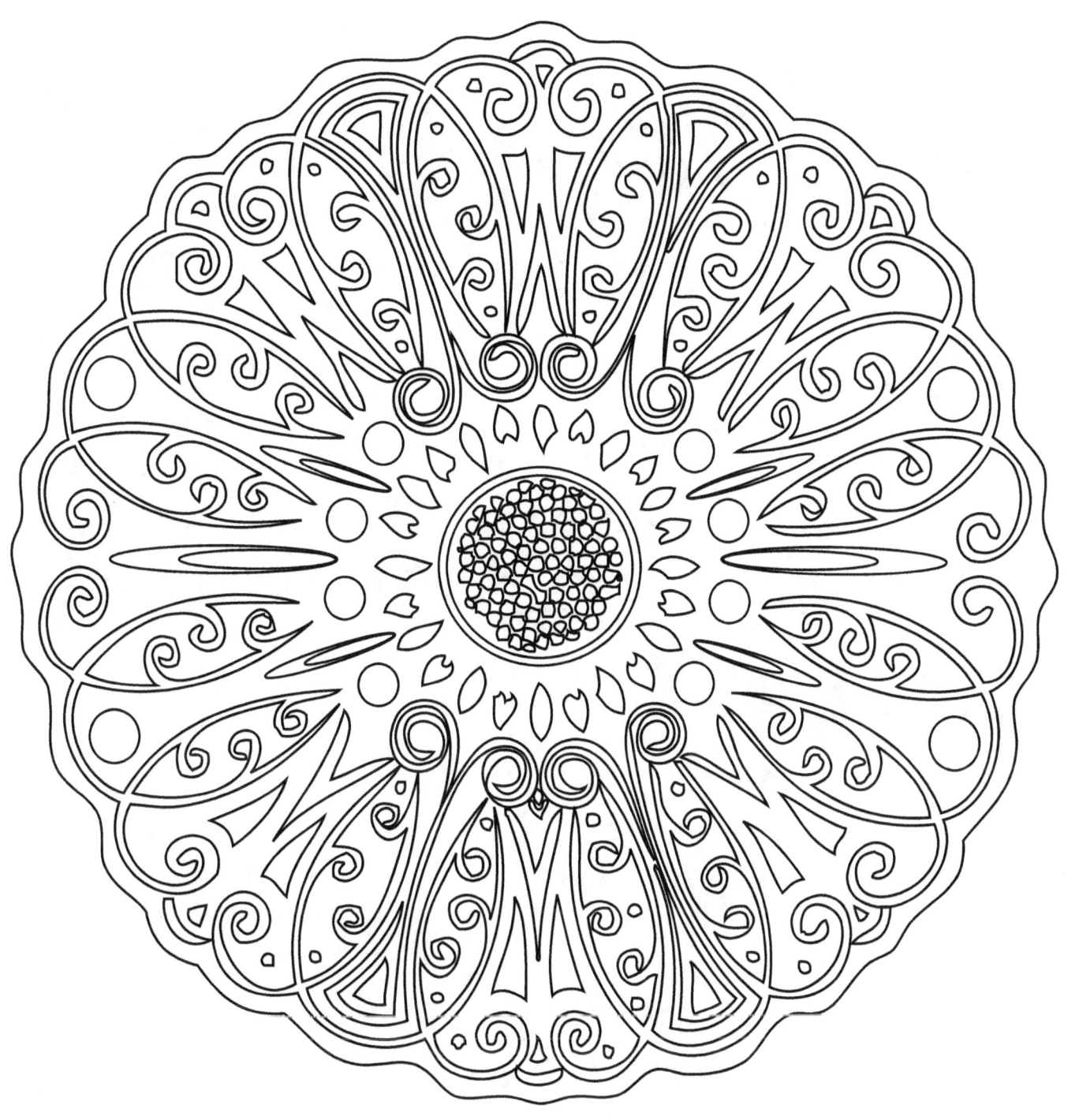

THE JOURNEY OF A THOUSAND MILES
BEGINS WITH ONE STEP.
- LAO TZU

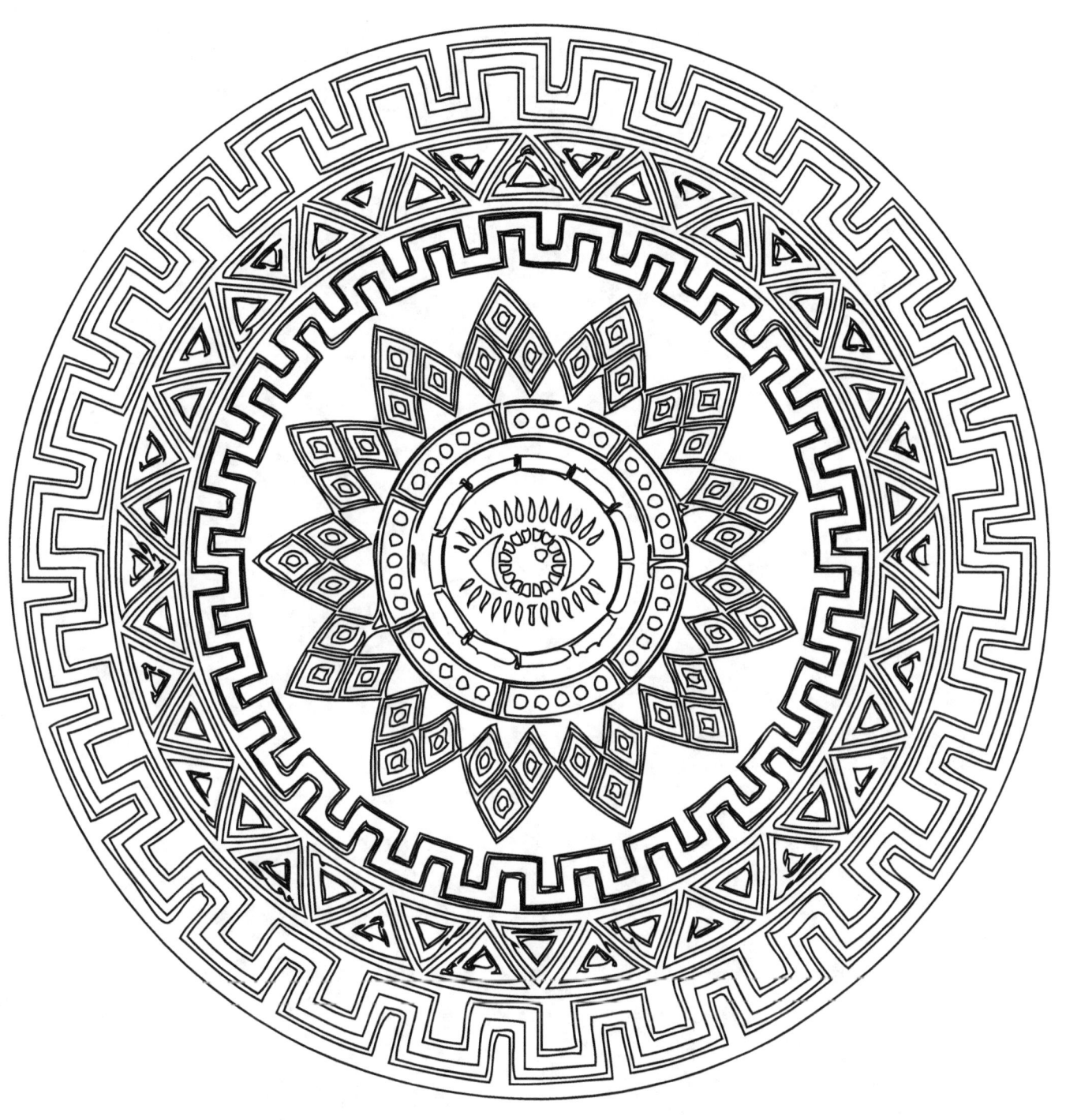

THE BEST REVENGE IS MASSIVE SUCCESS.
- FRANK SINATRA

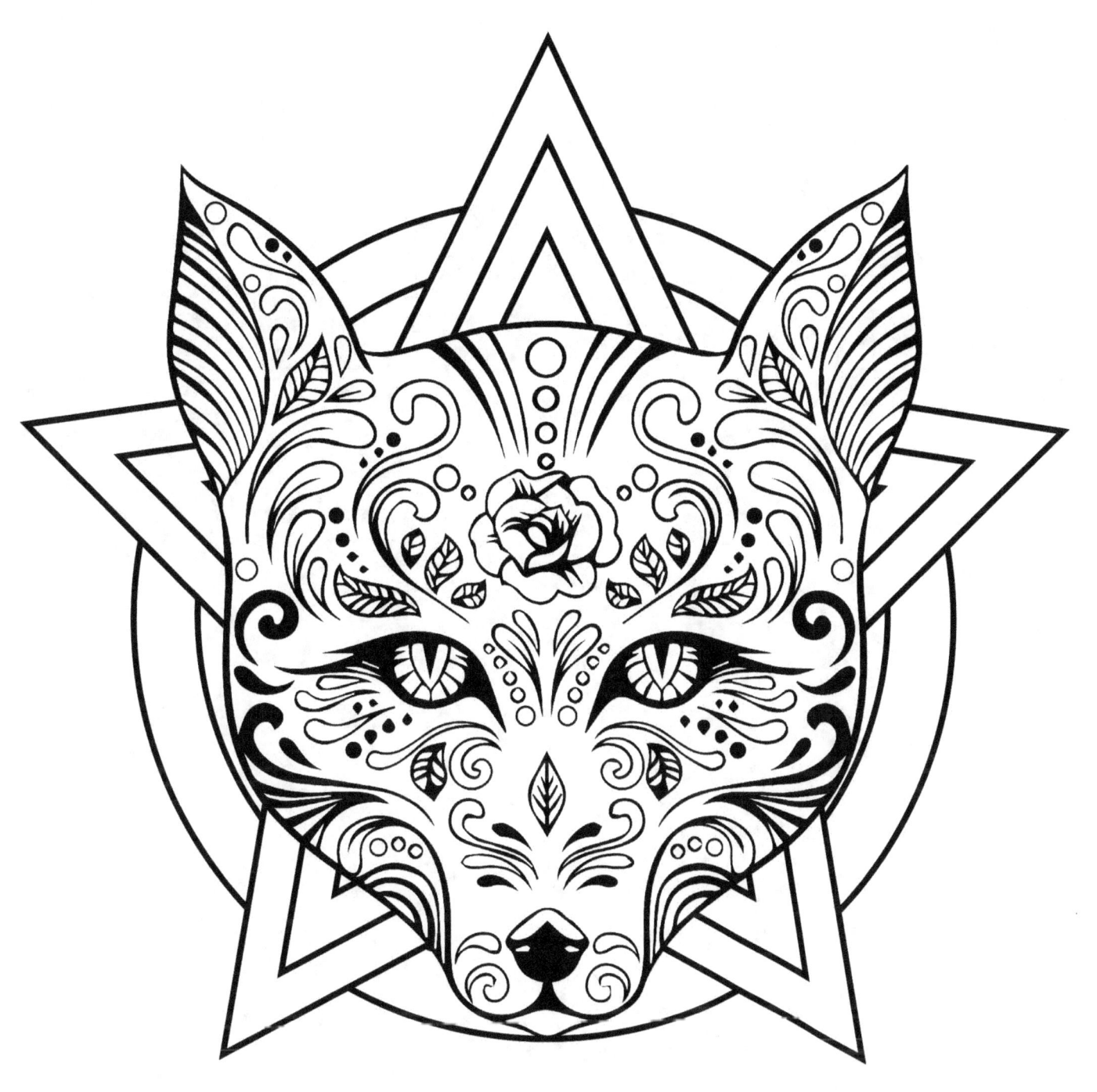

LIFE ITSELF IS YOUR TEACHER, AND YOU
ARE IN A STATE OF CONSTANT LEARNING.
- BRUCE LEE

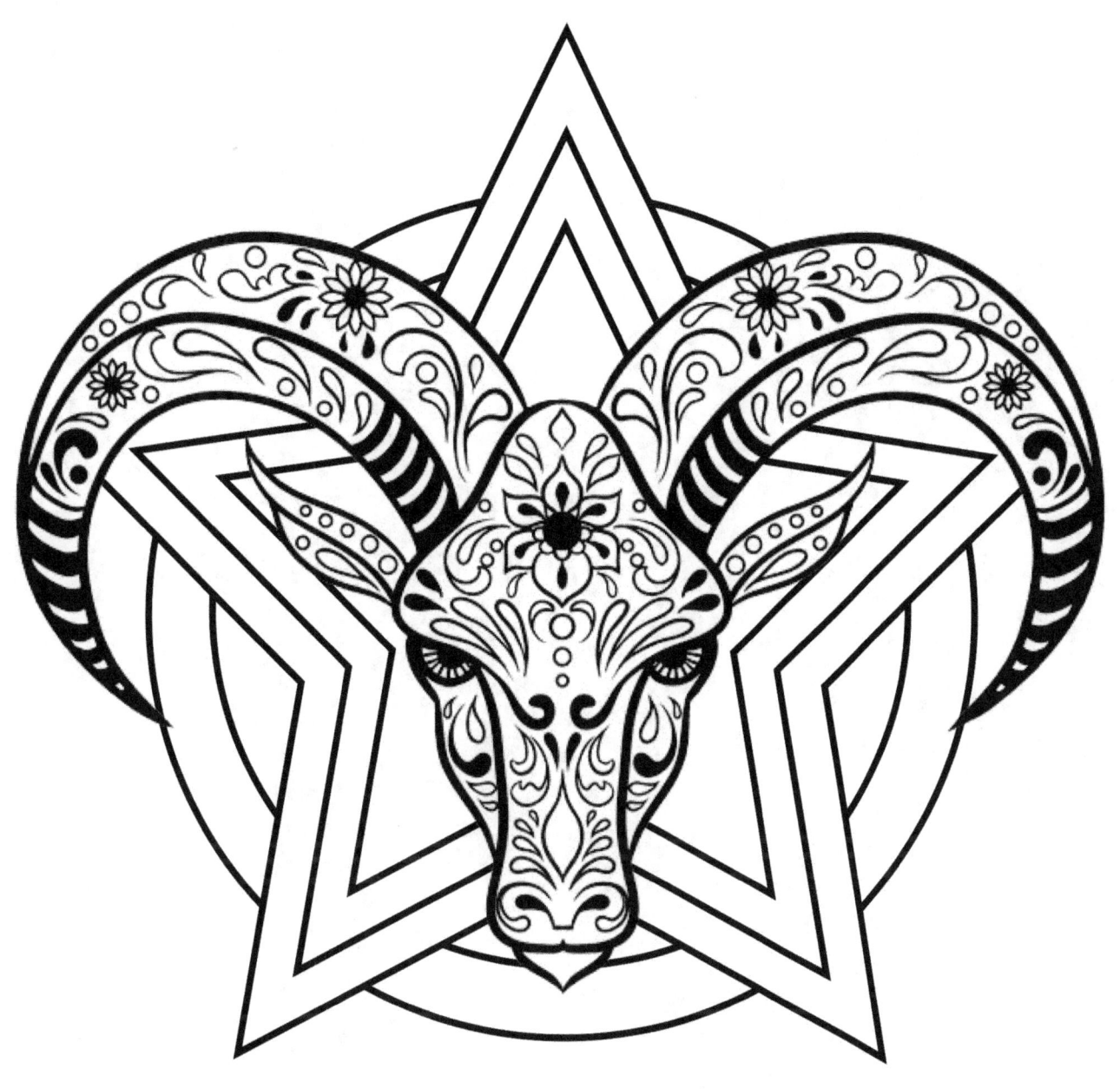

CHALLENGES ARE WHAT MAKE LIFE INTERESTING
AND OVERCOMING THEM IS
WHAT MAKES LIFE MEANINGFUL.
- JOSHUA J,. MARINE

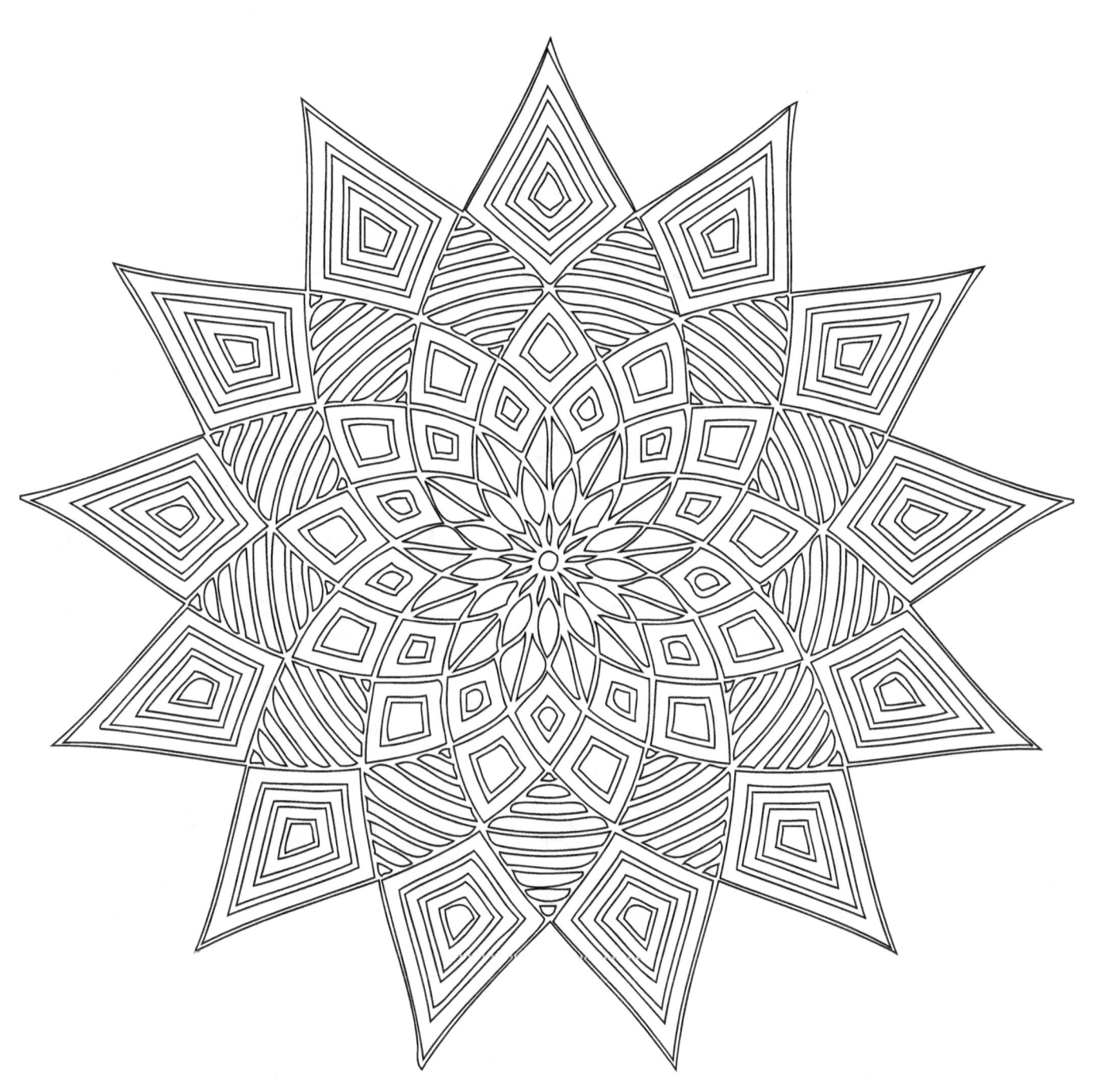

WE BECOME WHAT WE THINK ABOUT.
- EARL NIGHTINGALE

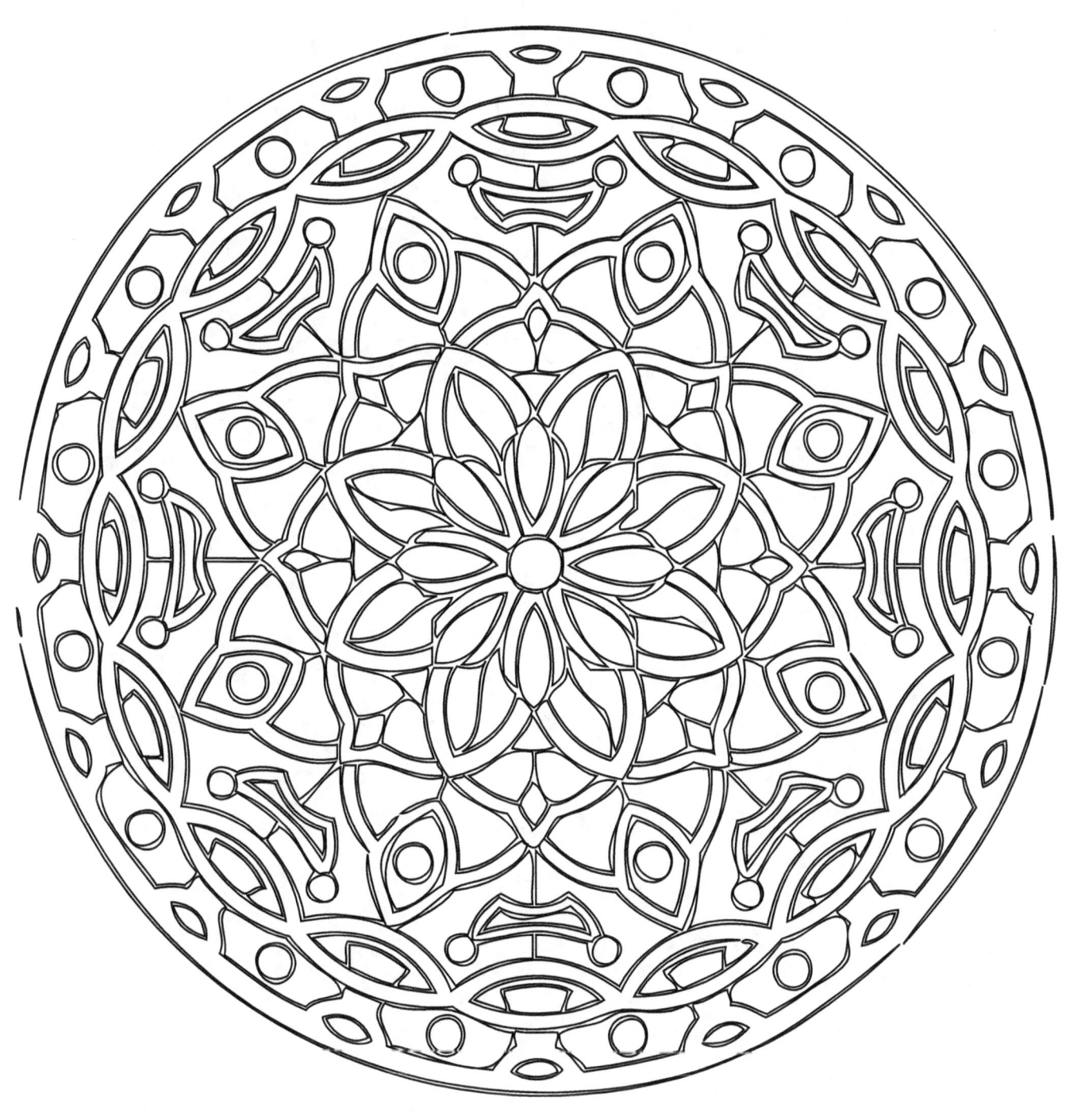

LIFE IS *WHAT* HAPPENS TO YOU *WHILE* YOU'RE BUSY MAKING OTHER PLANS. - JOHN LENNON

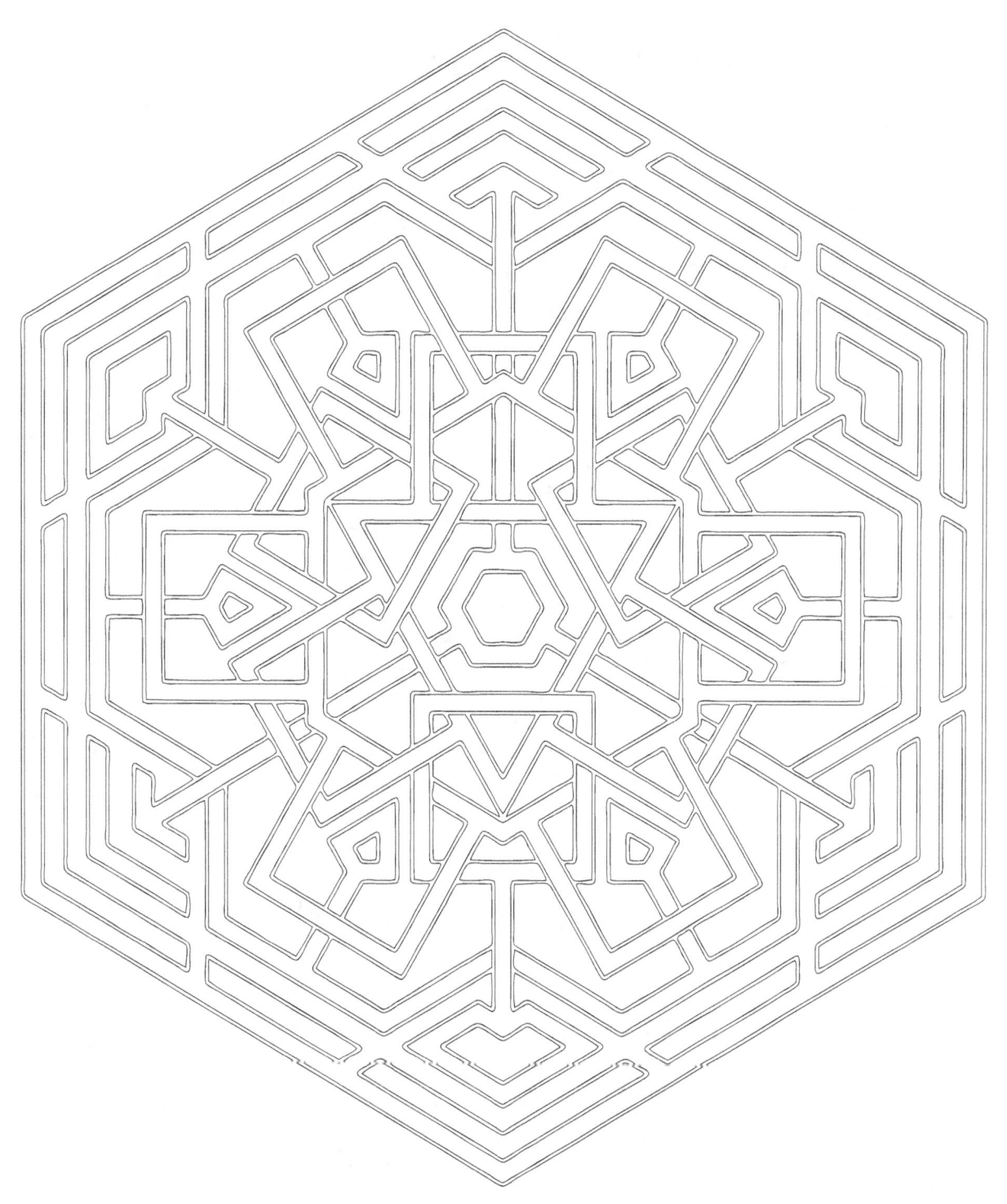

I AM NOT A PRODUCT OF MY CIRCUMSTANCES.
I AM A PRODUCT OF MY DECISIONS.
- STEPHEN COVEY

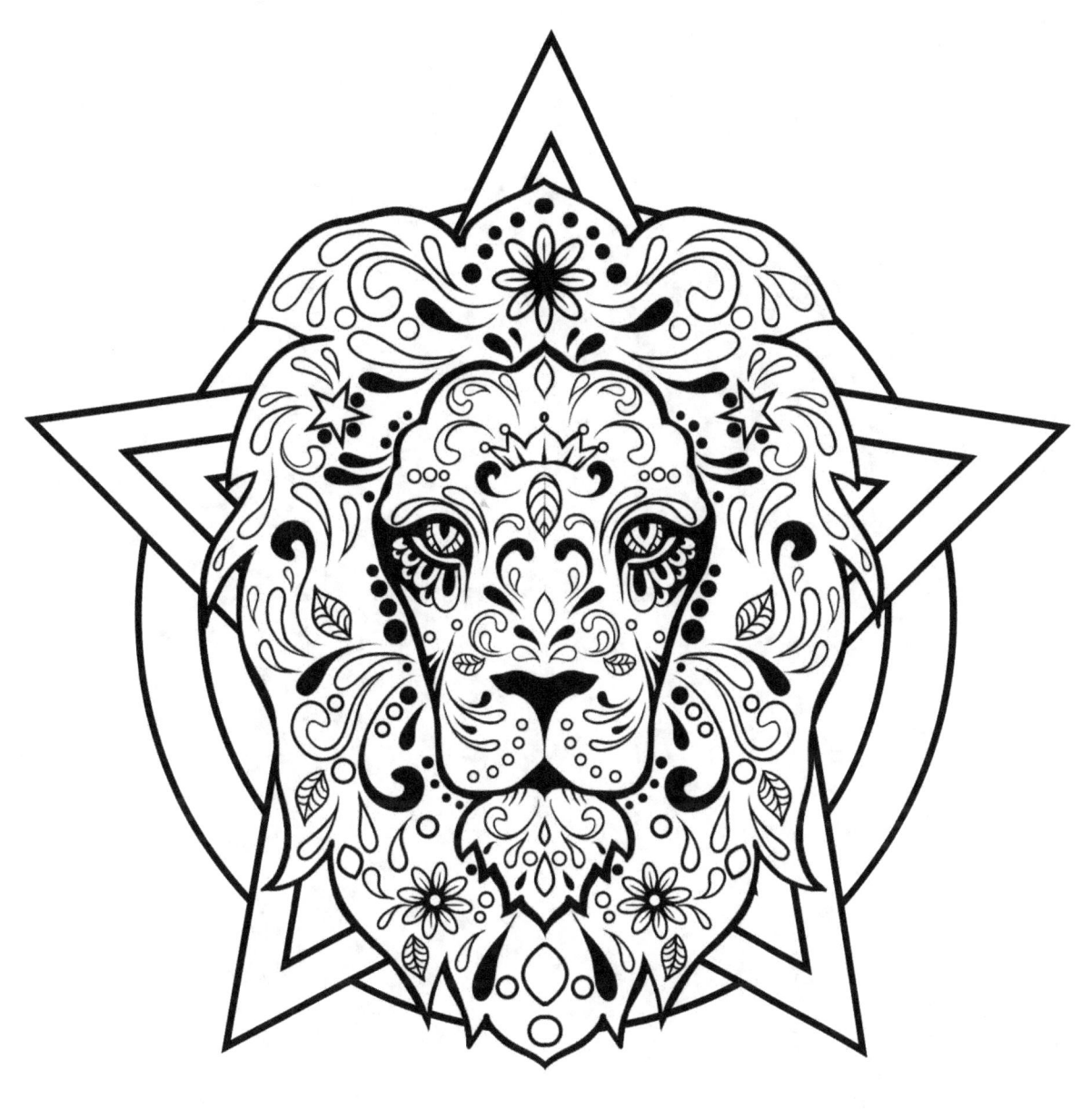

AN OBSTACLE IS OFTEN A STEPPING STONE.
- PRESCOTT

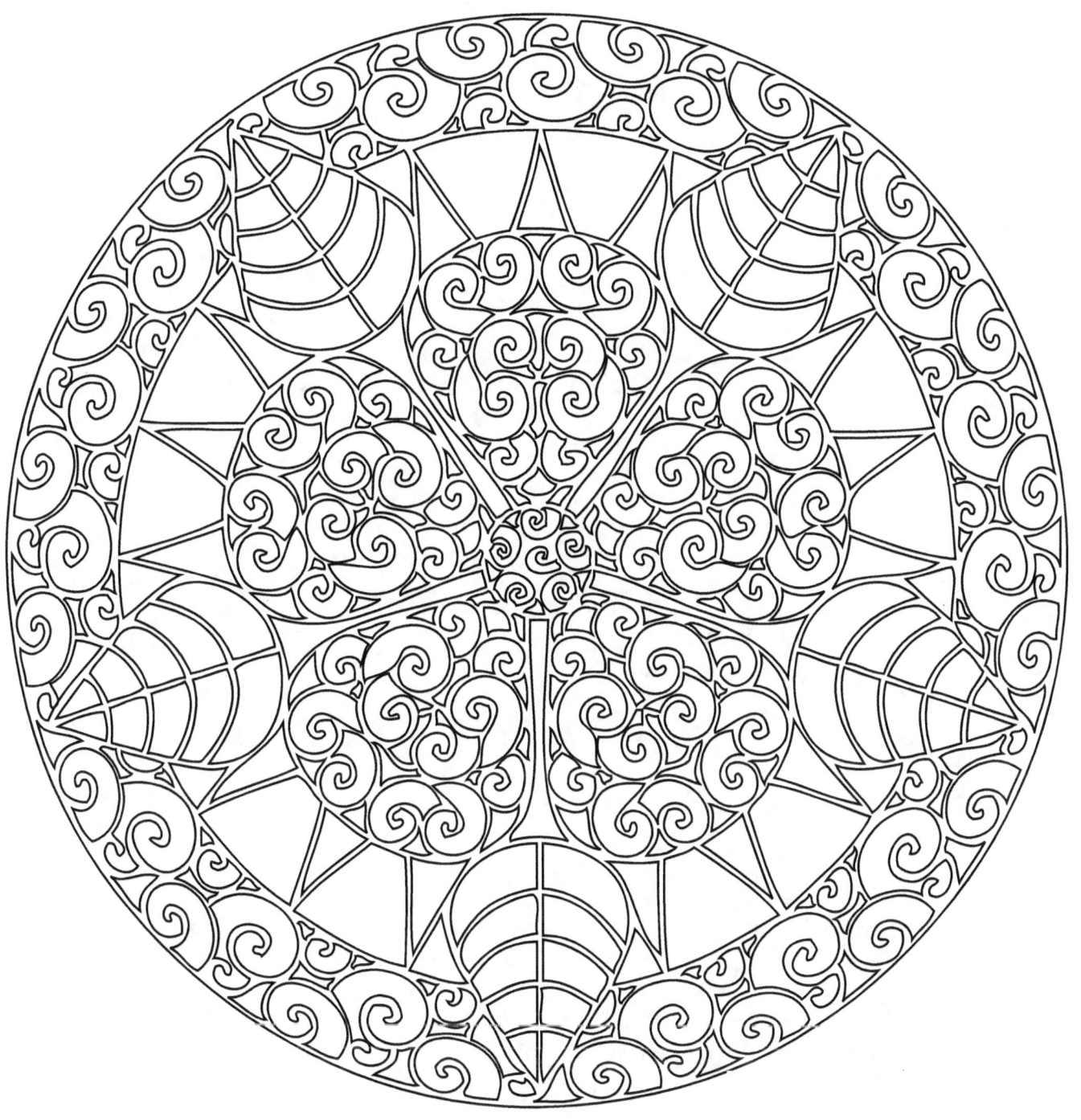

EDUCATION COSTS MONEY.
BUT THEN SO DOES IGNORANCE..
- SIR CLAUS MOSER

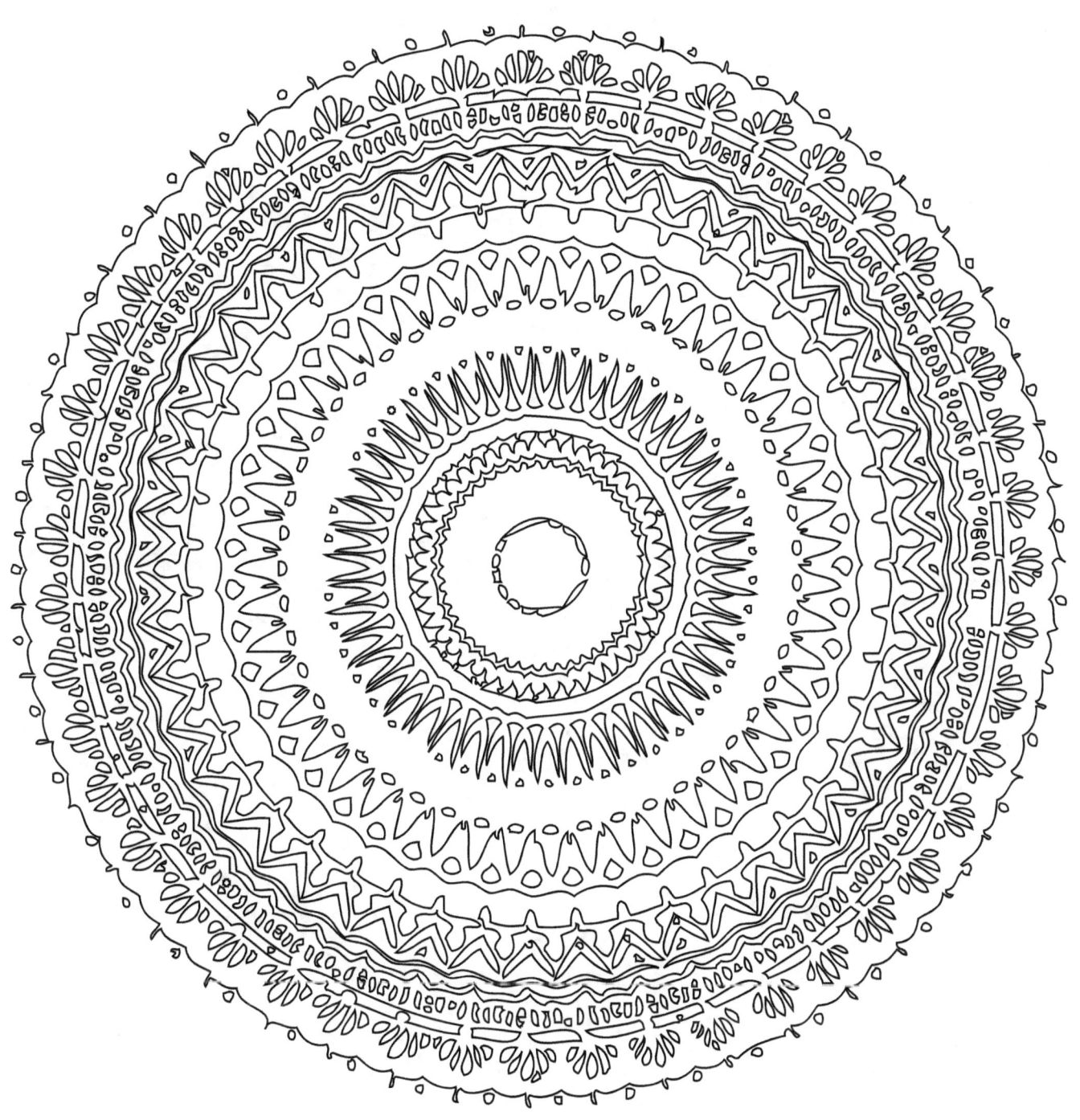

EITHER YOU RUN THE DAY, OR THE DAY RUNS YOU.
- JIM ROHN

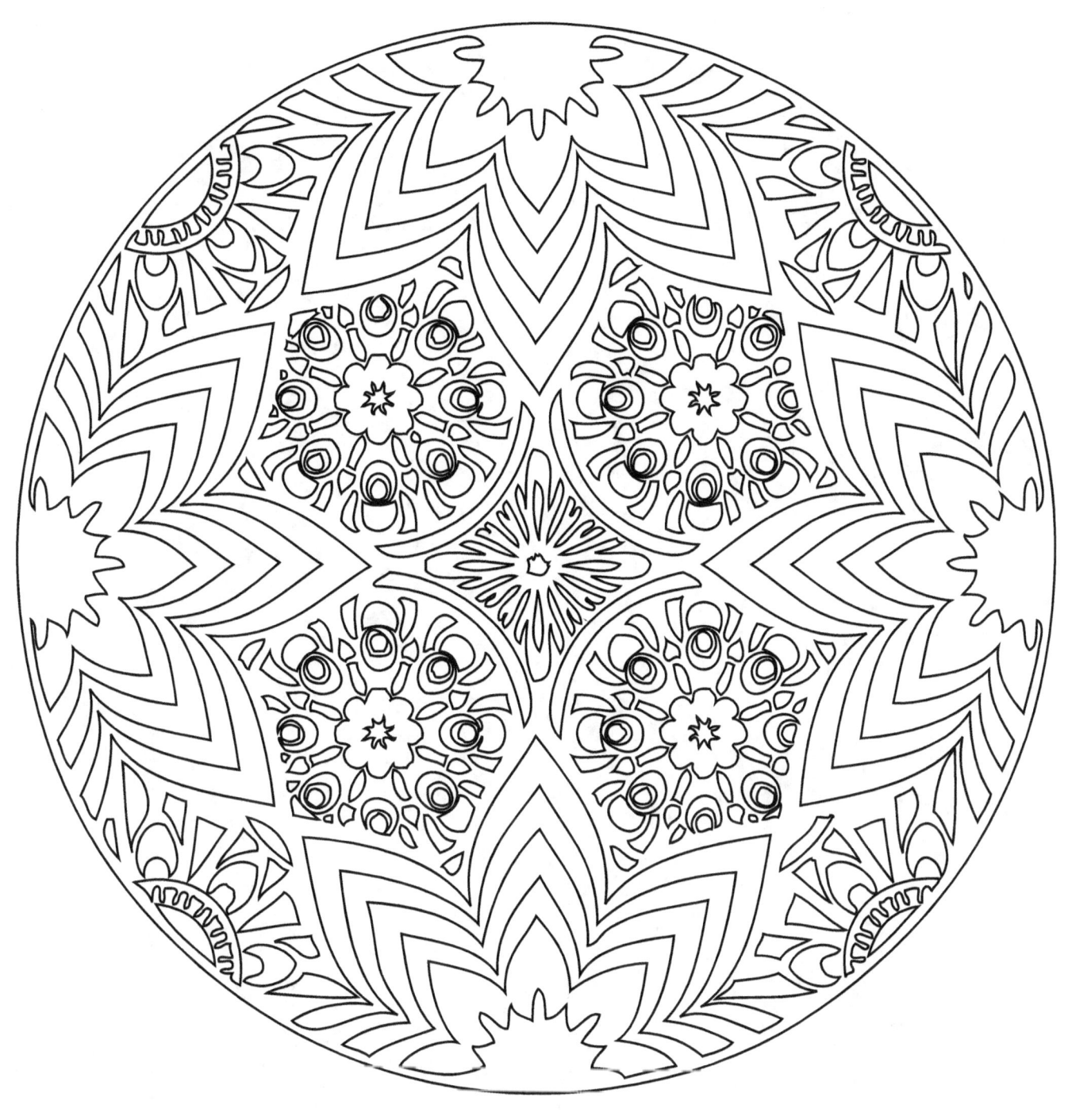

NURTURE YOUR MIND WITH GREAT THOUGHTS.
TO BELIEVE IN THE HEROIC MAKES HEROES.
- BENJAMIN DISRAELI

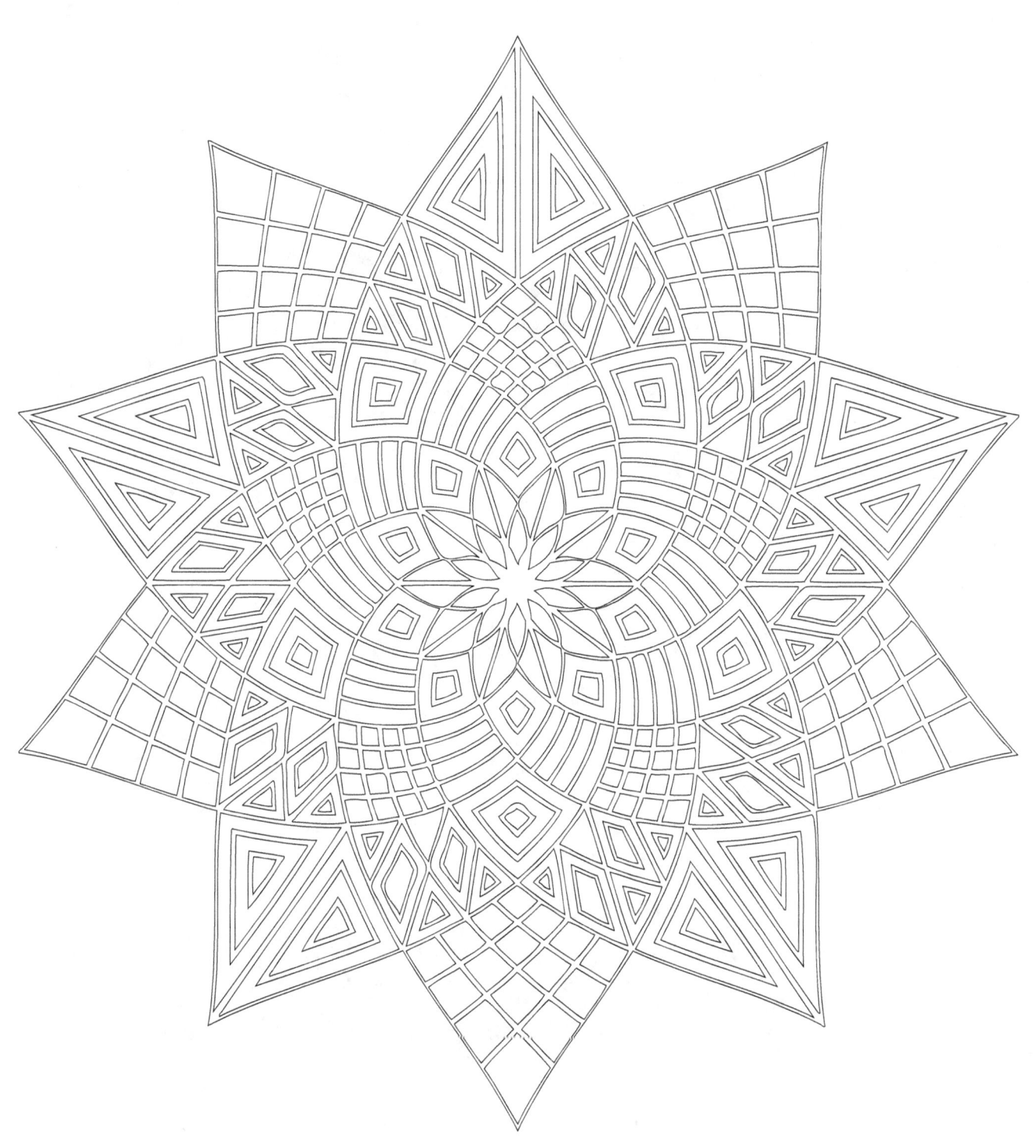

YOU ONLY LIVE ONCE, BUT IF YOU DO IT RIGHT,
ONCE IS ENOUGH.
- MAE WEST

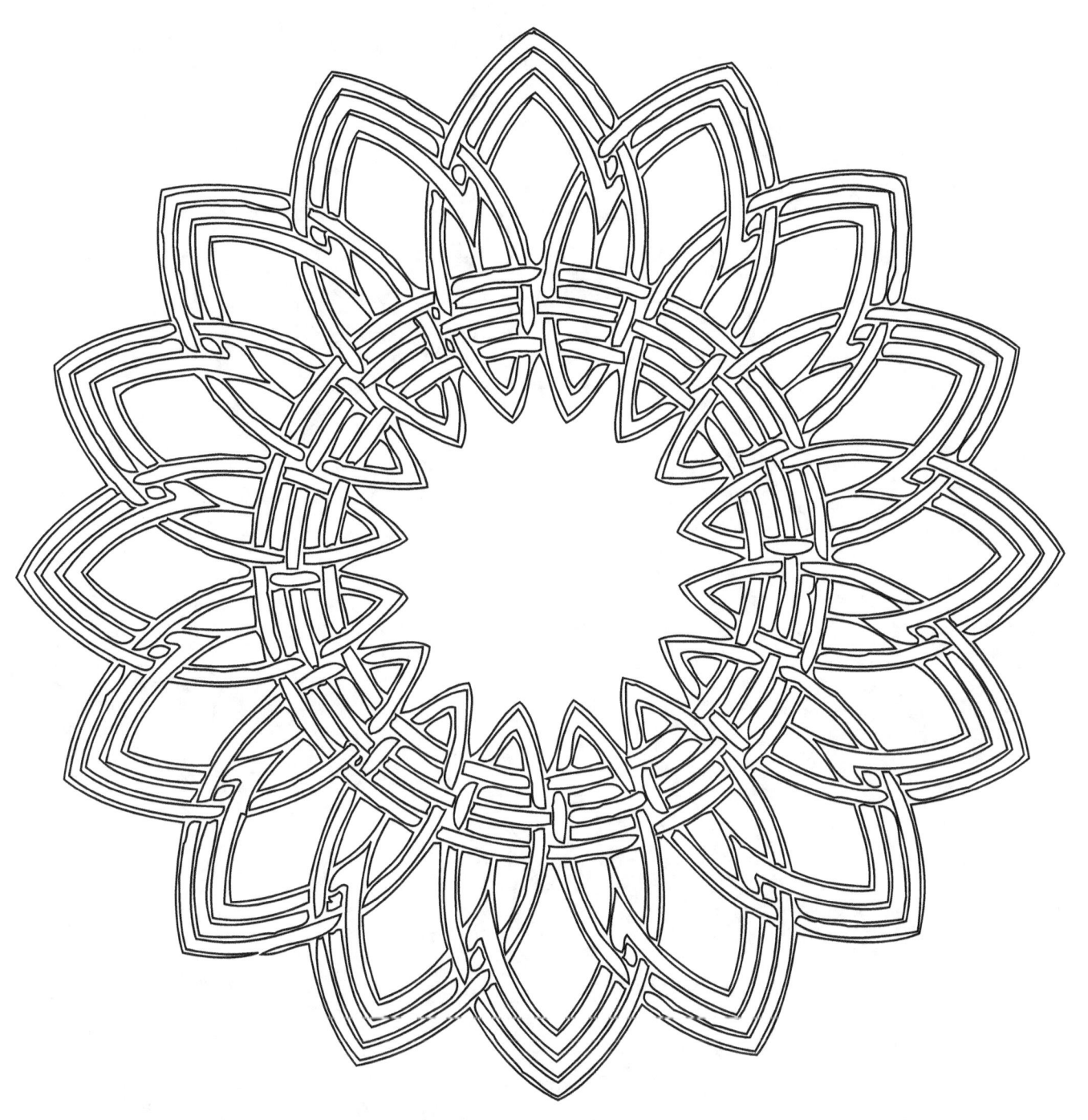

TO LIVE IS THE RAREST THING IN THE WORLD.
MOST PEOPLE EXIST, THAT IS ALL.
- OSCAR WILDE

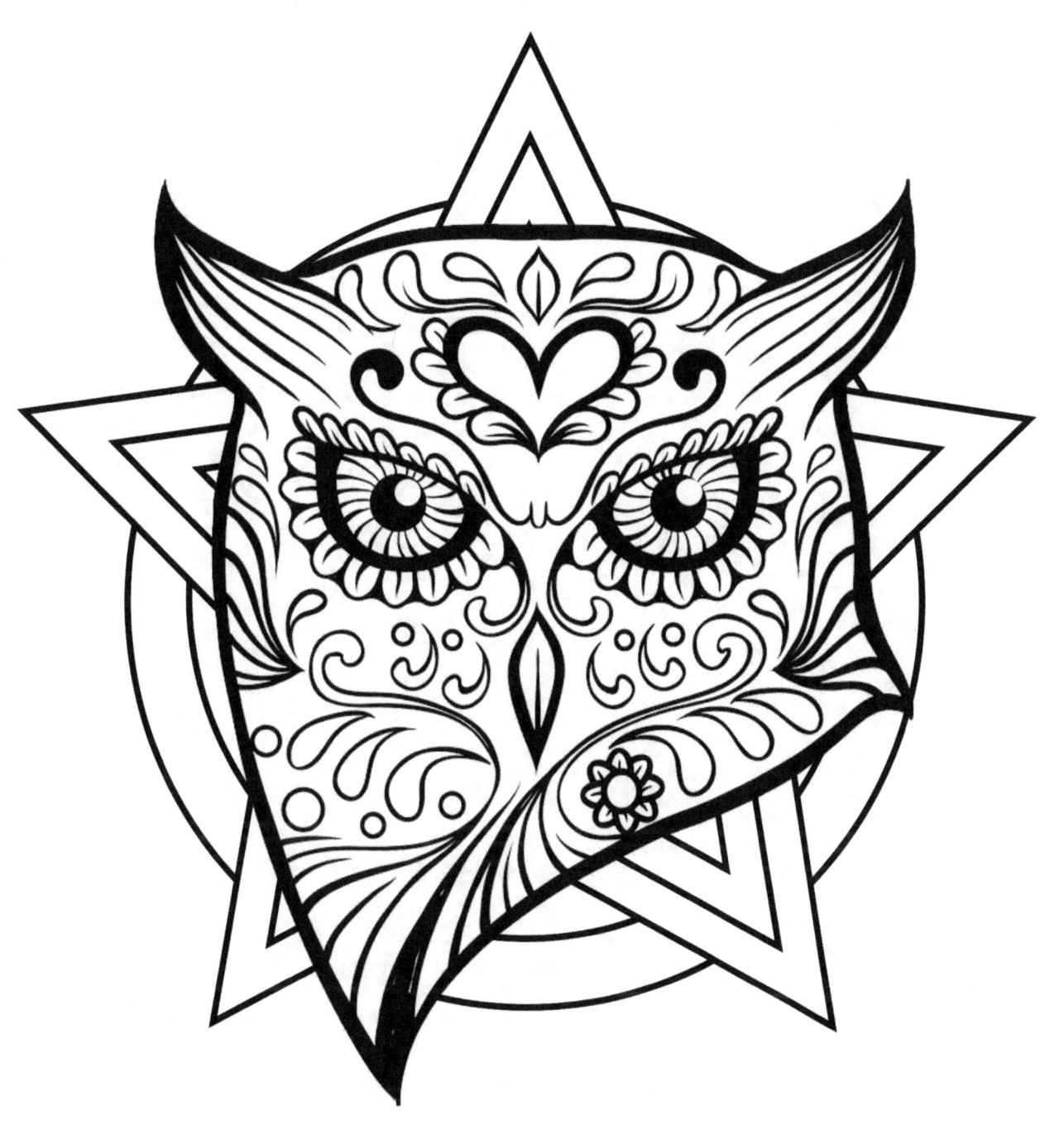

BE EVERYTHING YOU CAN IMAGINE IS REAL.
- PABLO PICASSO

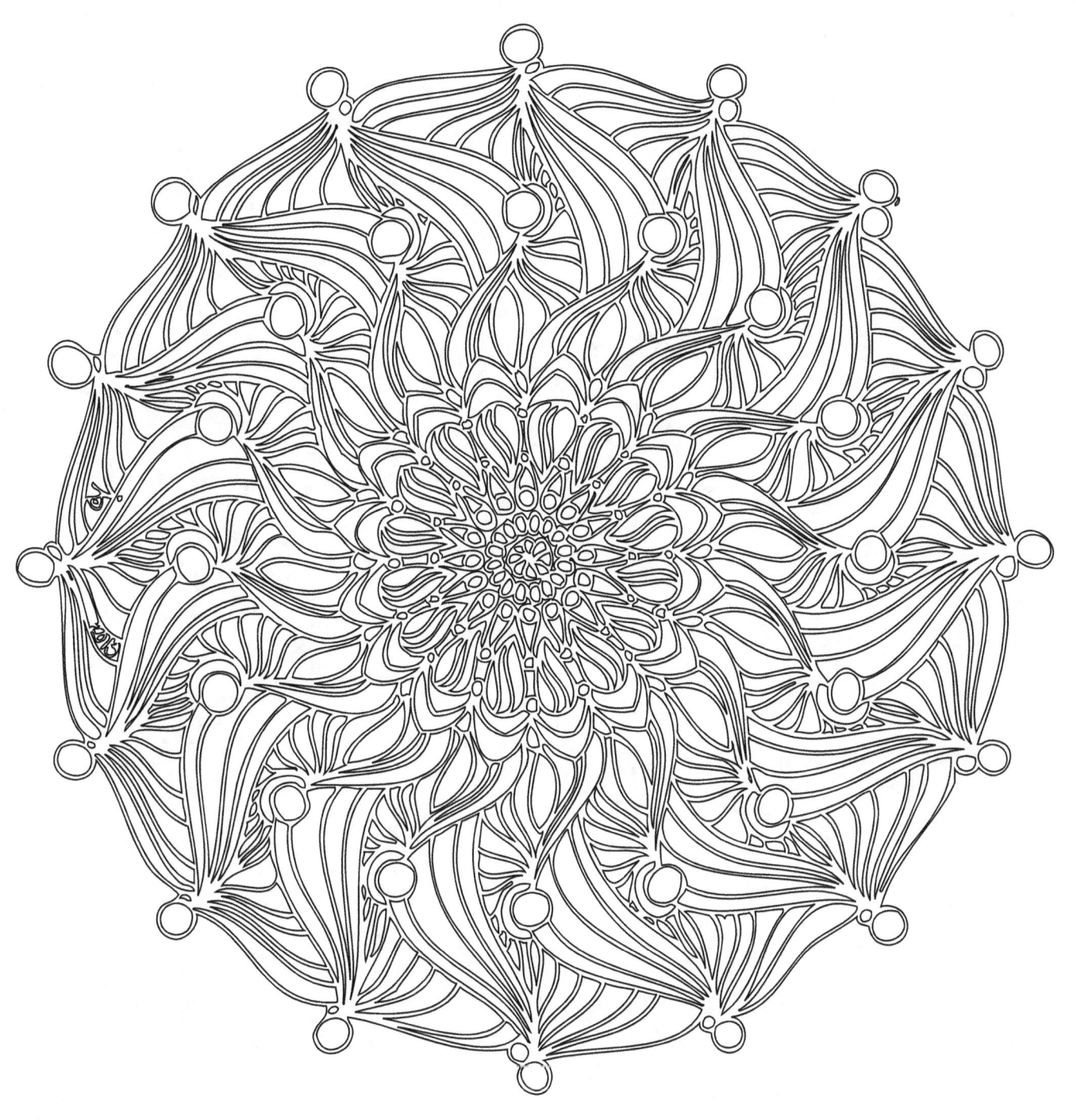

LIFE IS LIKE RIDING A BICYCLE.
TO KEEP YOUR BALANCE, YOU MUST
KEEP MOVING.
- ALBERT EINSTEIN

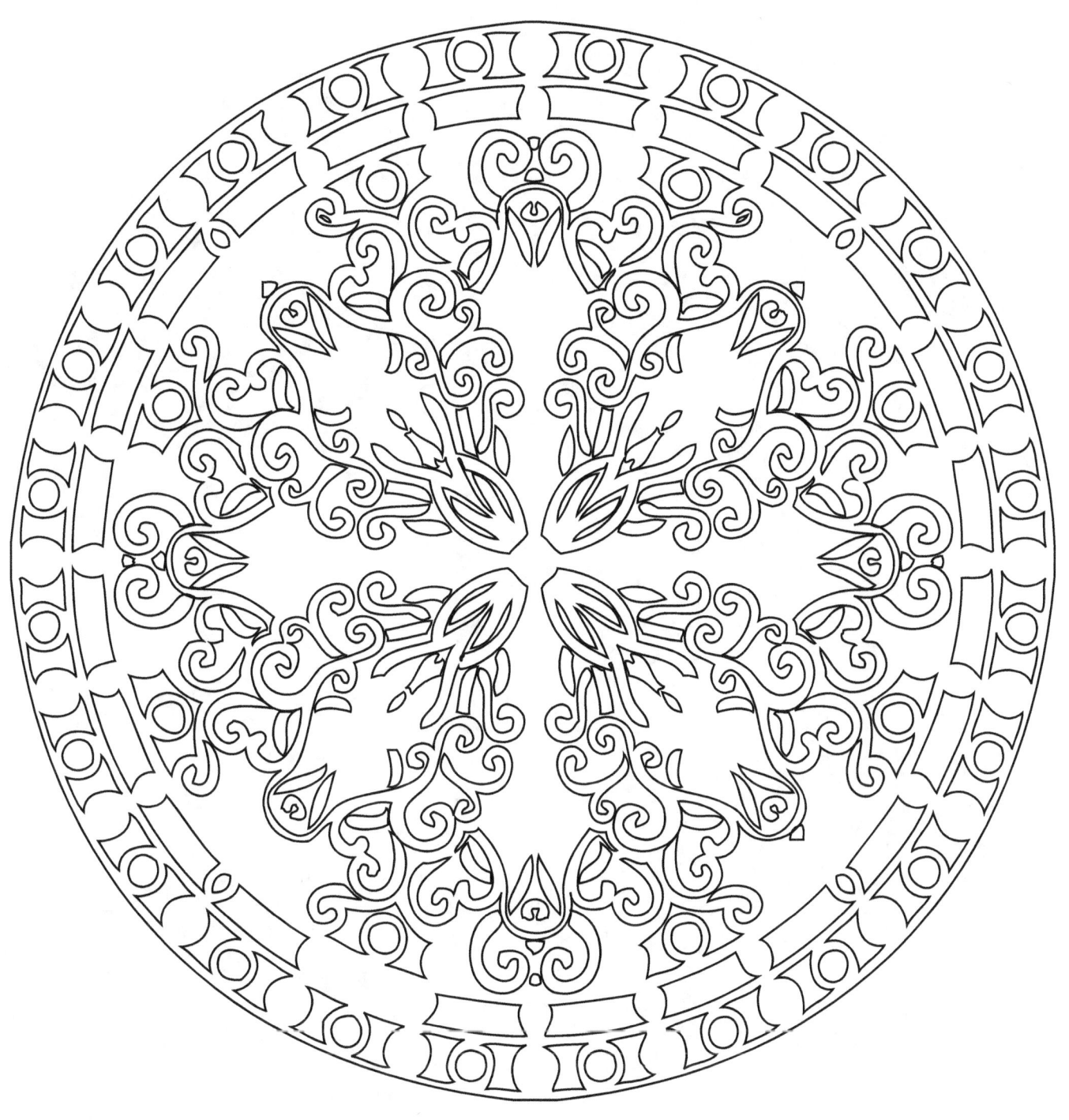

HARDSHIPS OFTEN PREPARE ORDINARY PEOPLE
FOR AN EXTRAORDINARY DESTINY.
- C.S LEWIS

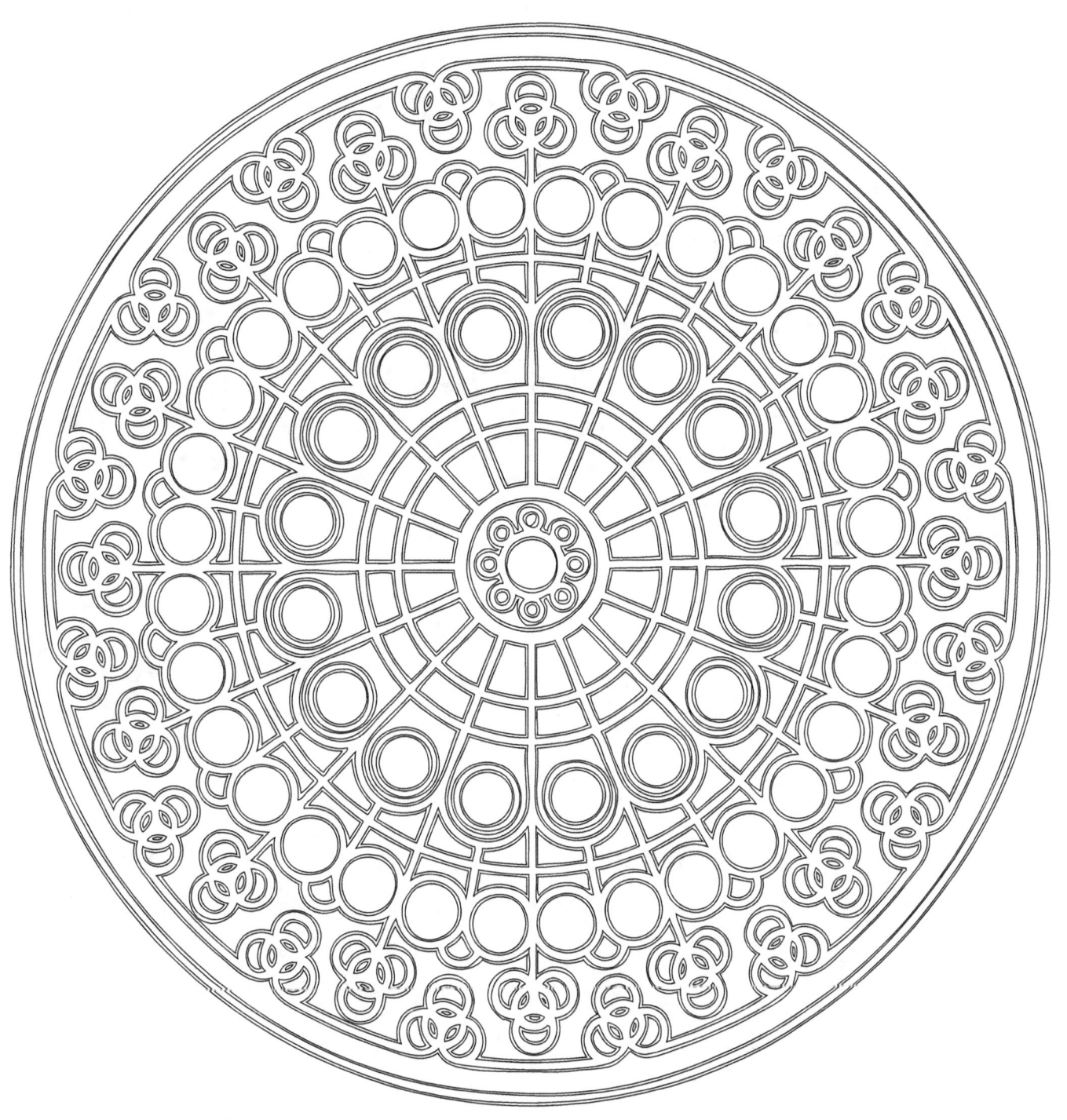

BE SO GOOD, THEY CAN'T IGNORE YOU
- STEVE MARTIN

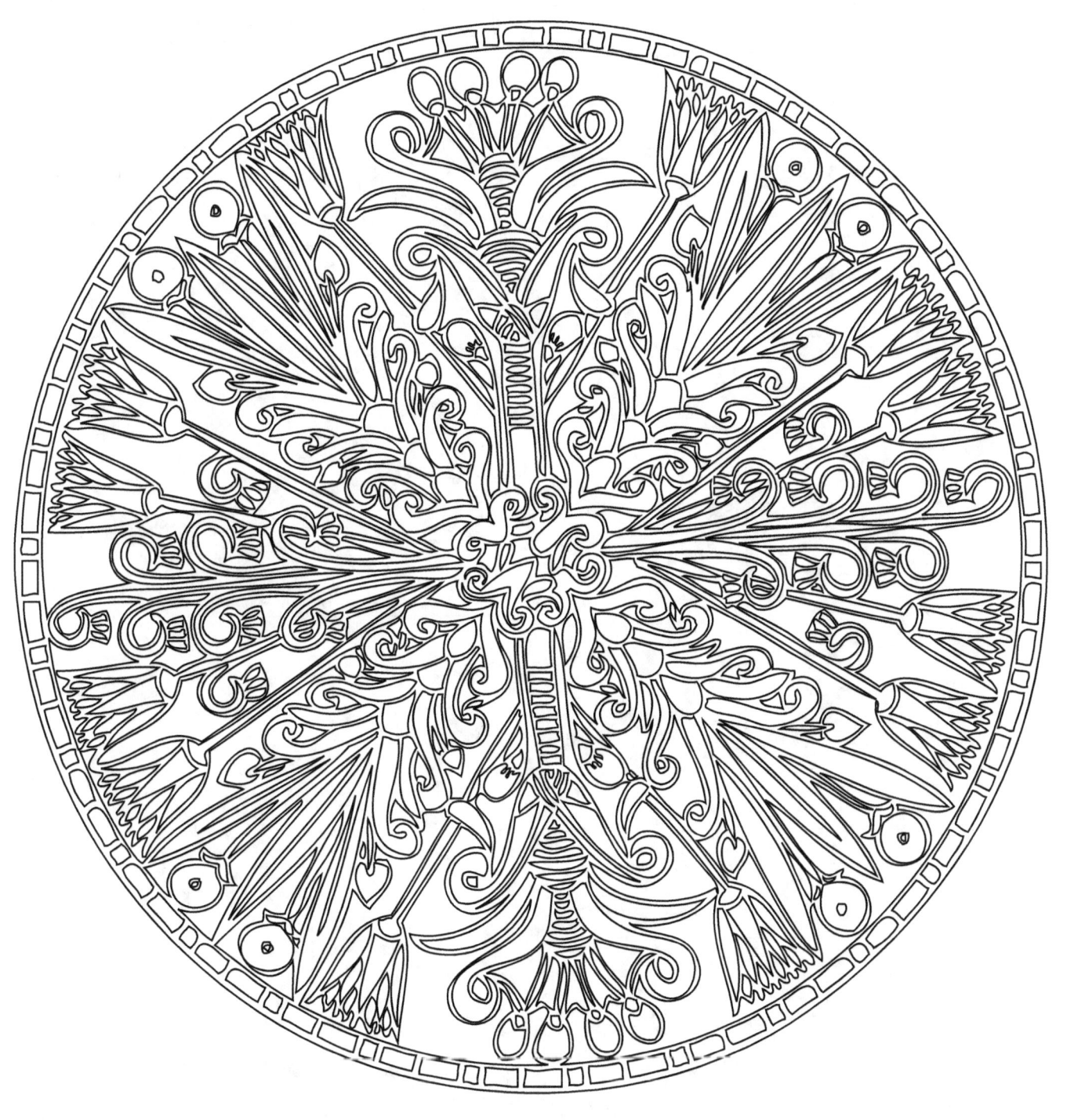

OUR GREATEST WEAKNESS LIES
IN GIVING UP.
- THOMAS A. EDISON

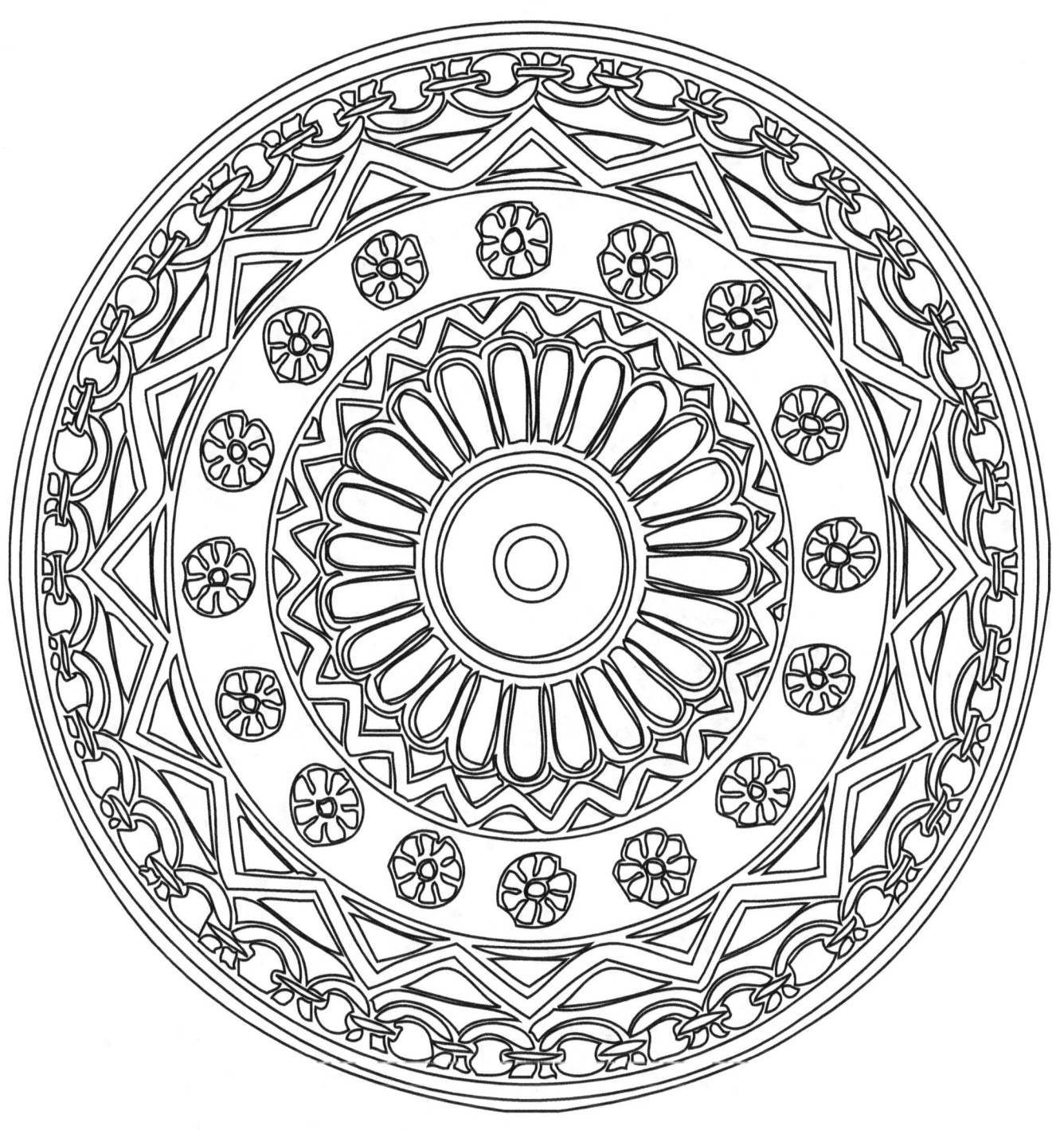

WHEN THE POWER OF LOVE OVERCOMES
THE LOVE OF POWER, THE WORLD WILL
KNOW PEACE.
- THOMAS A. EDISON

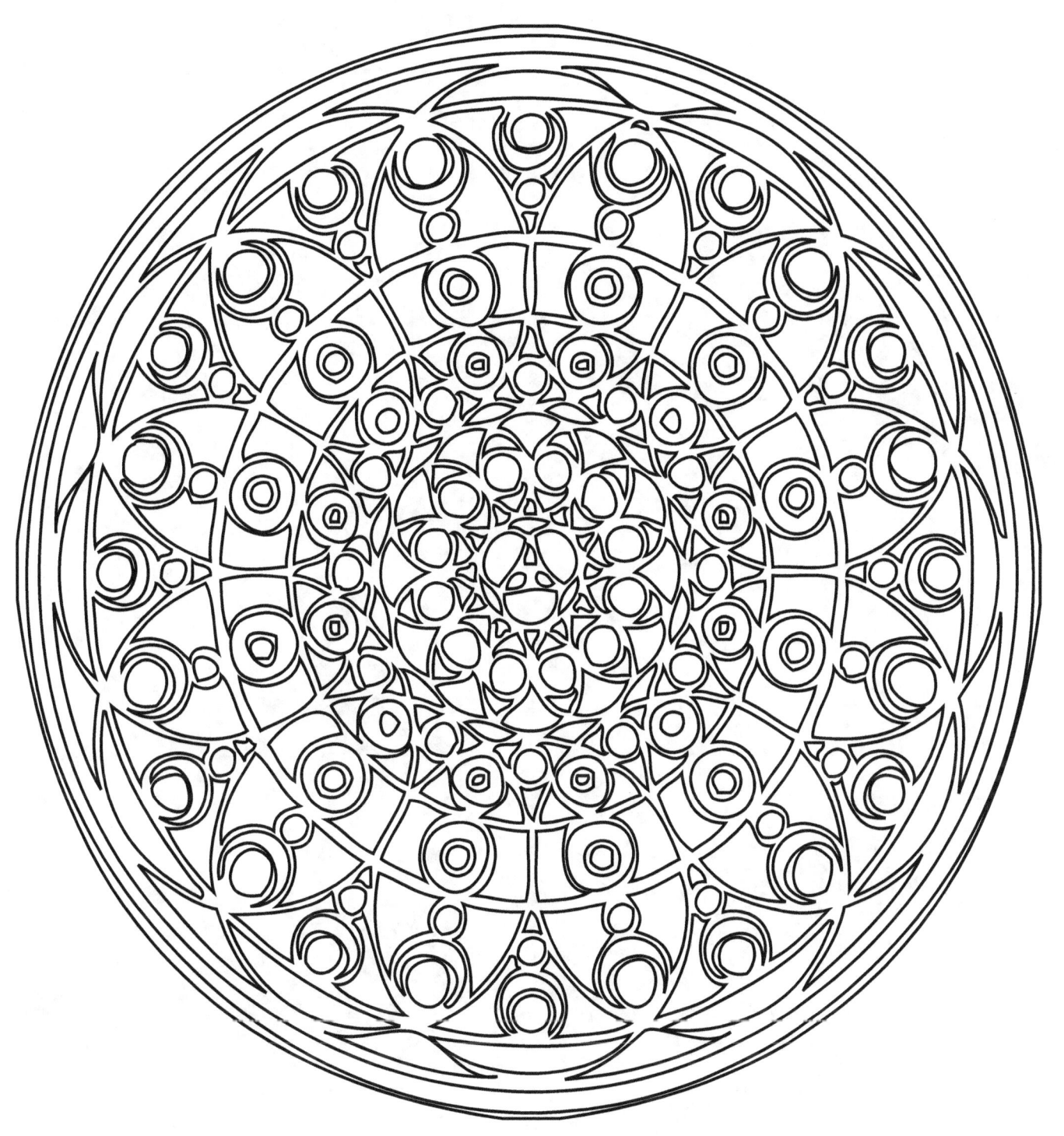

TO BE A CHAMP, YOU HAVE TO BELIEVE IN
YOURSELF, WHEN NOBODY ELSE WILL.
- SUGAR RAY ROBINSON

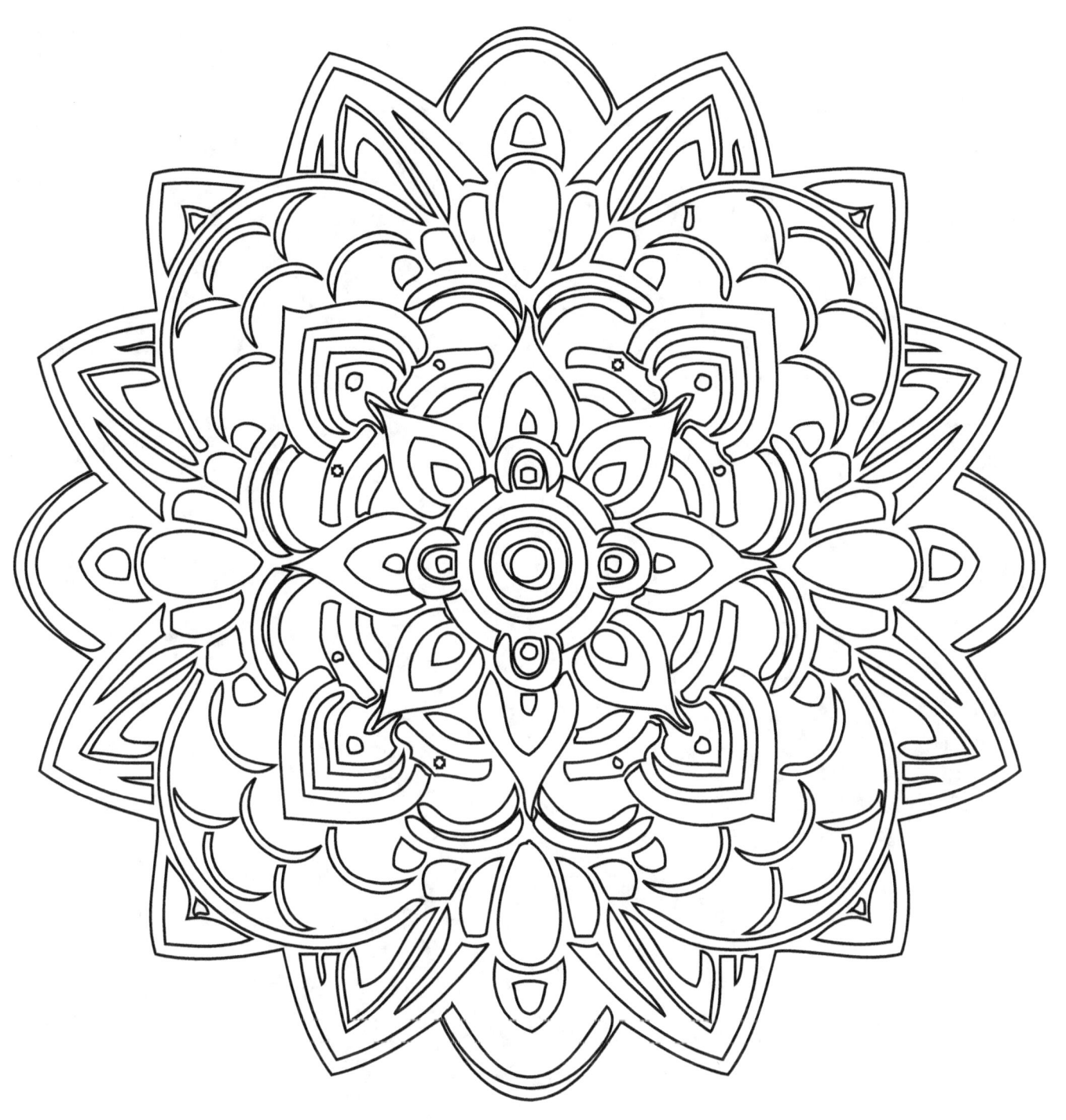

IT IS NEVER TOO LATE TO BE WHO YOU MIGHT
HAVE BEEN.
- GEORGE ELLIOT

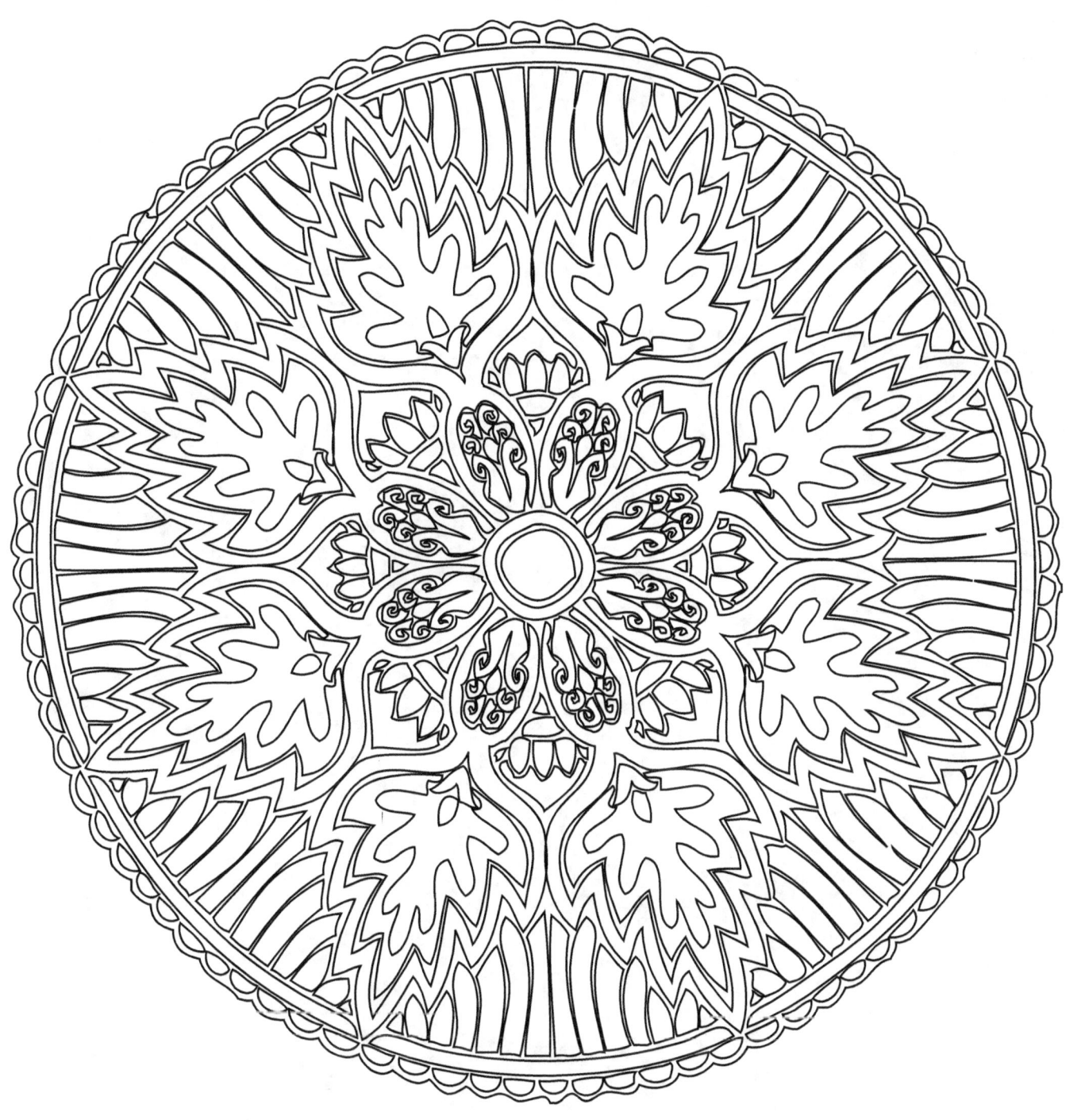

WHEN YOU ARE GOING THROUGH HELL,
KEEP GOING...
- WINSTON CHURCHILL

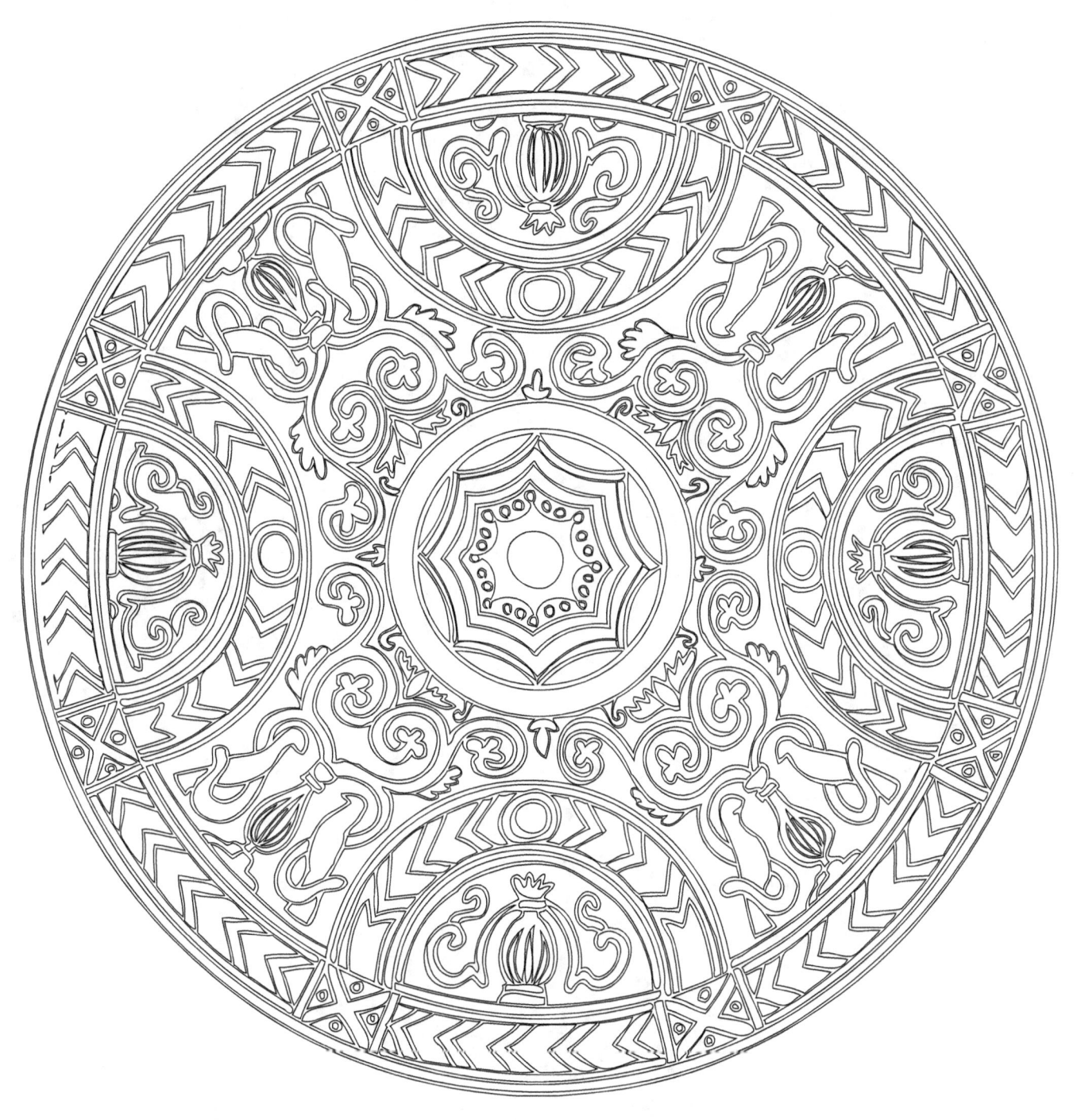

DON'T *WASTE* YOUR TIME *WITH* EXPLANATIONS,
PEOPLE ONLY *WANT* TO HEAR *WHAT*
THEY *WANT* TO HEAR.
- PAULO COELHO

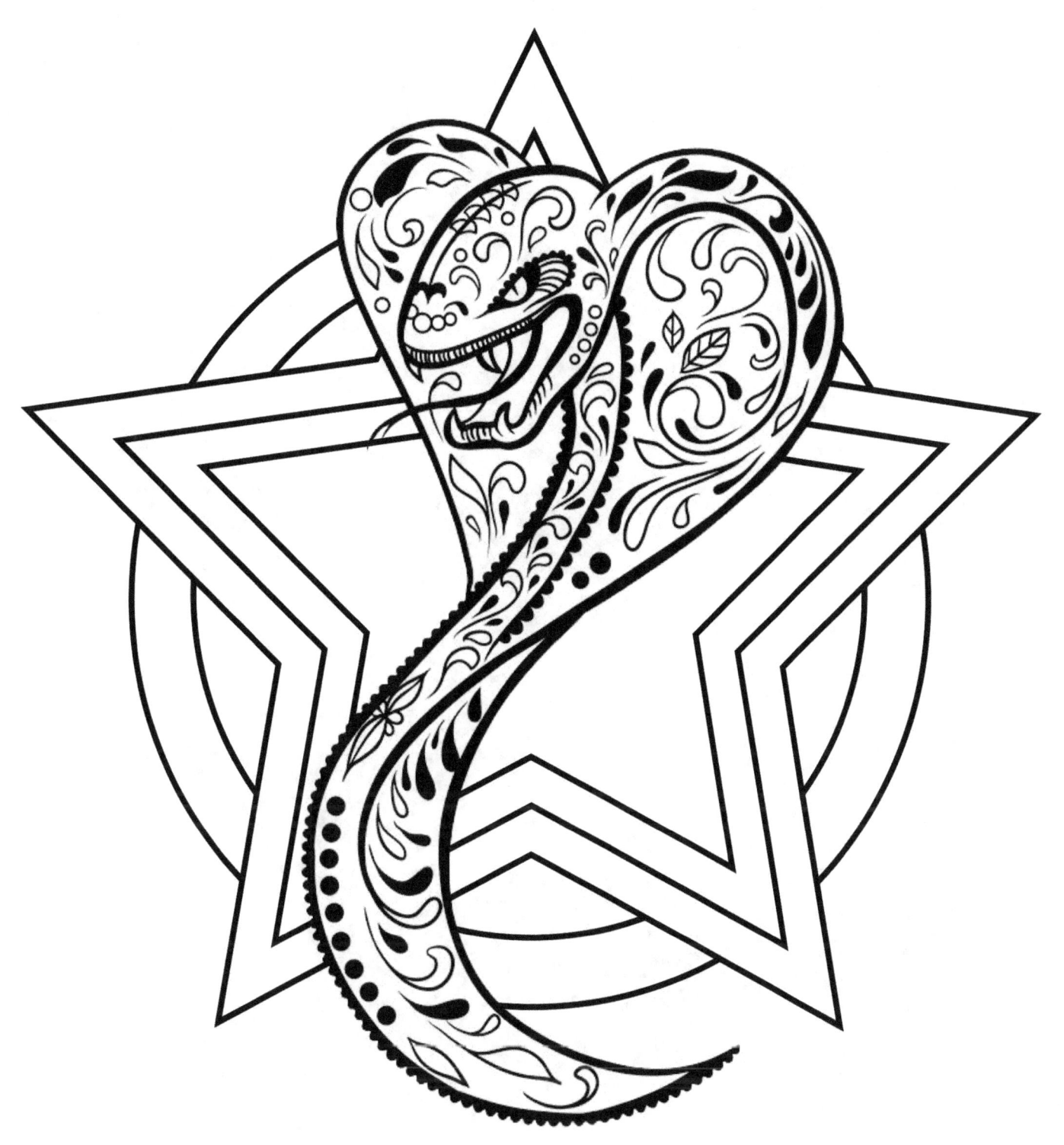

WHATEVER THE MIND OF MAN CAN CONCEIVE
AND BELIEVE, IT CAN ACHIEVE.
- NAPOLEON HILL

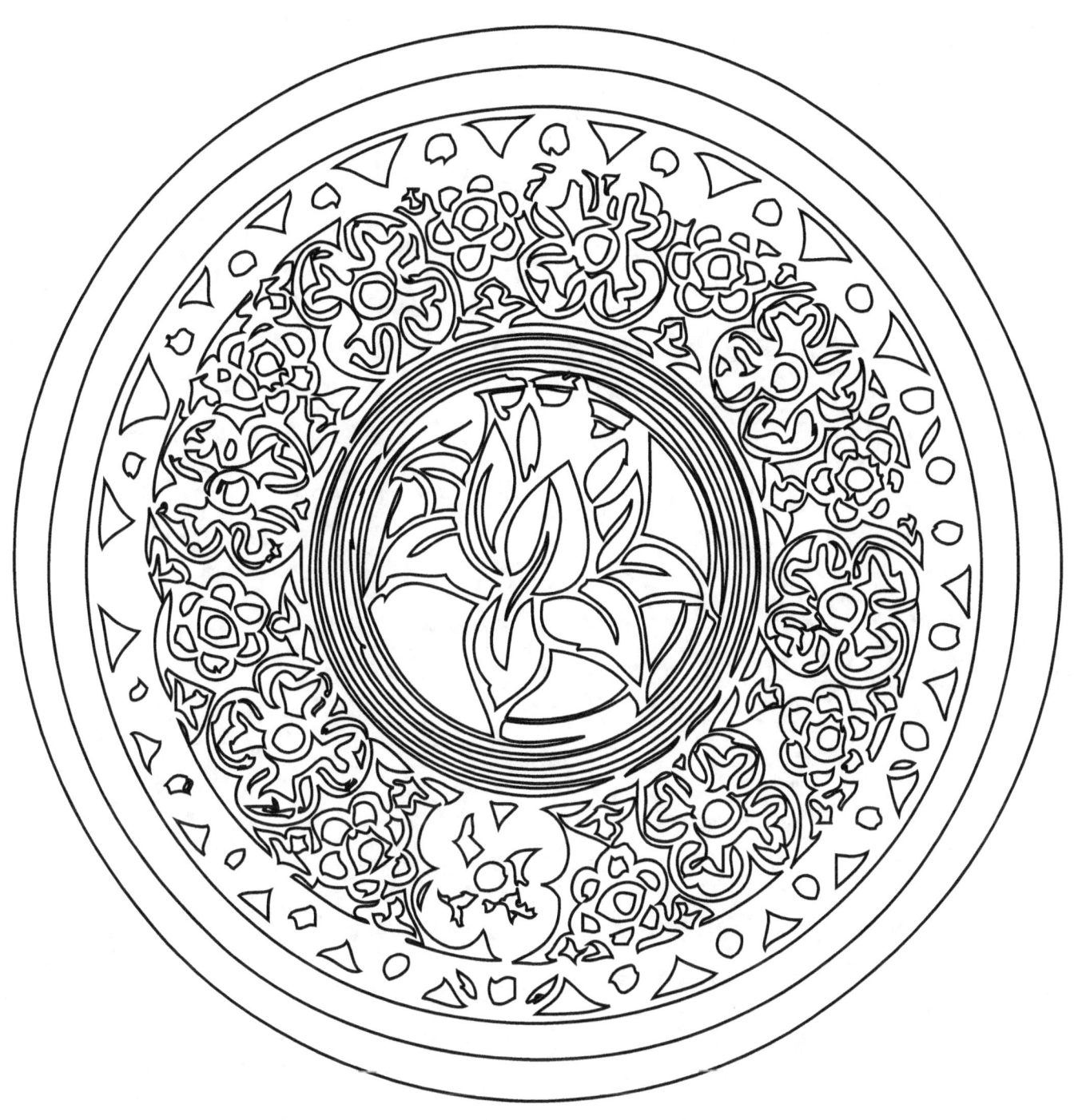

EVERY CHILD IS AN ARTIST.
THE PROBLEM IS HOW TO REMAIN
AN ARTIST ONCE HE GROWS UP.
- PABLO PICASSO

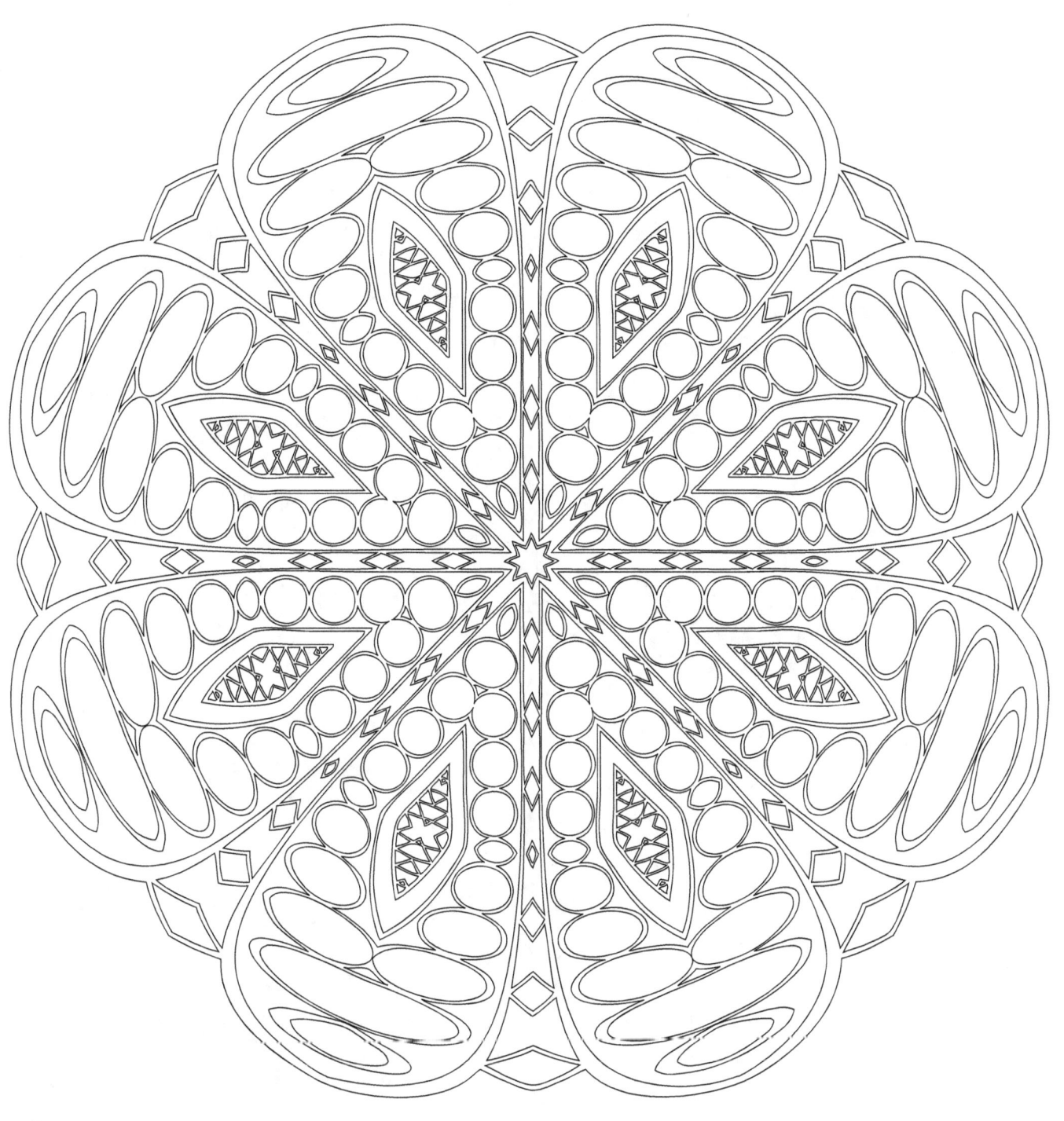

SOMETIMES GOOD THINGS FALL APART SO
BETTER THINGS CAN FALL TOGETHER.
- MARILYN MONROE

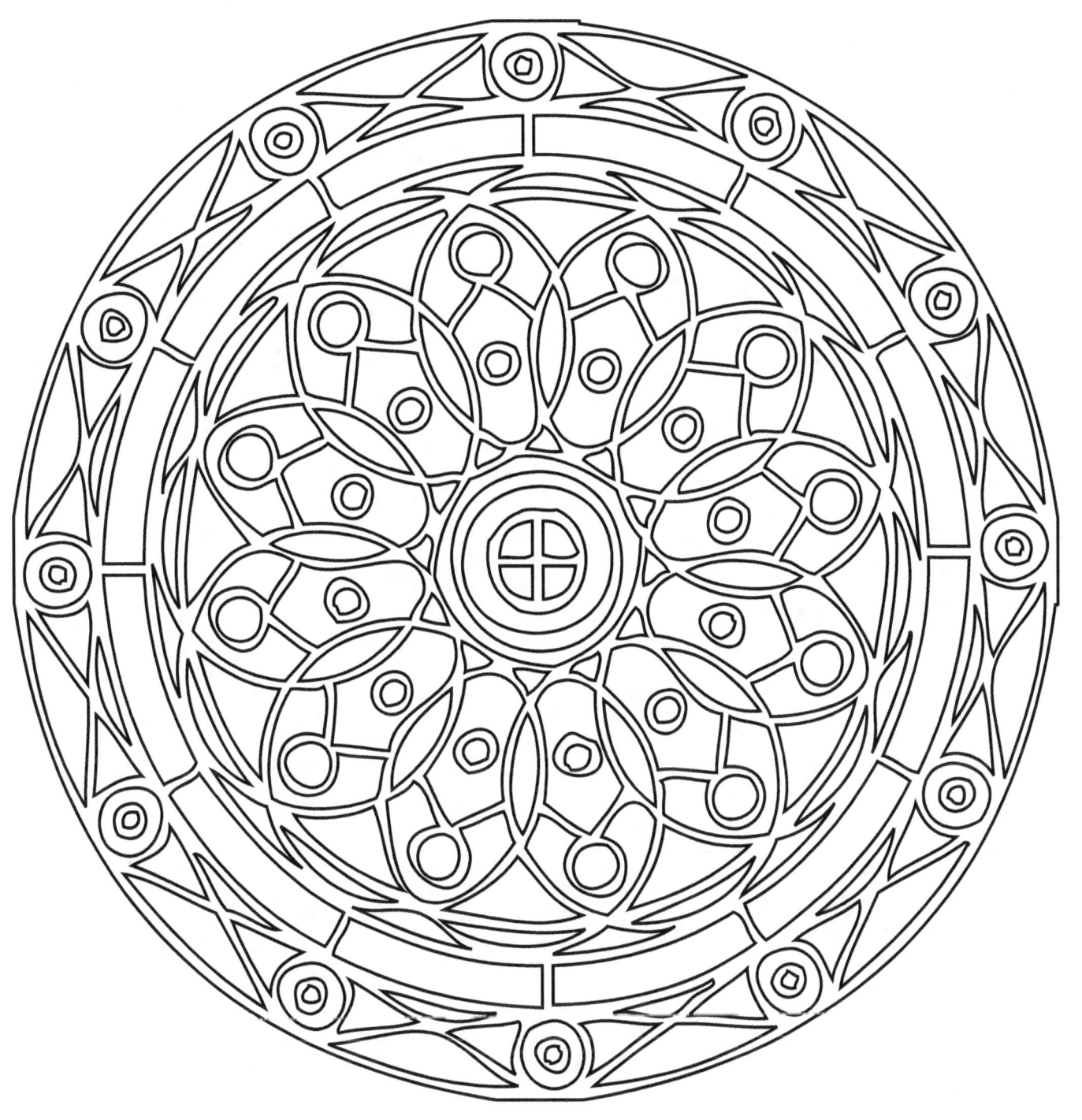

UNEARNED SUFFERING IS REDEMPTIVE.
- MARTIN LUTHER KING

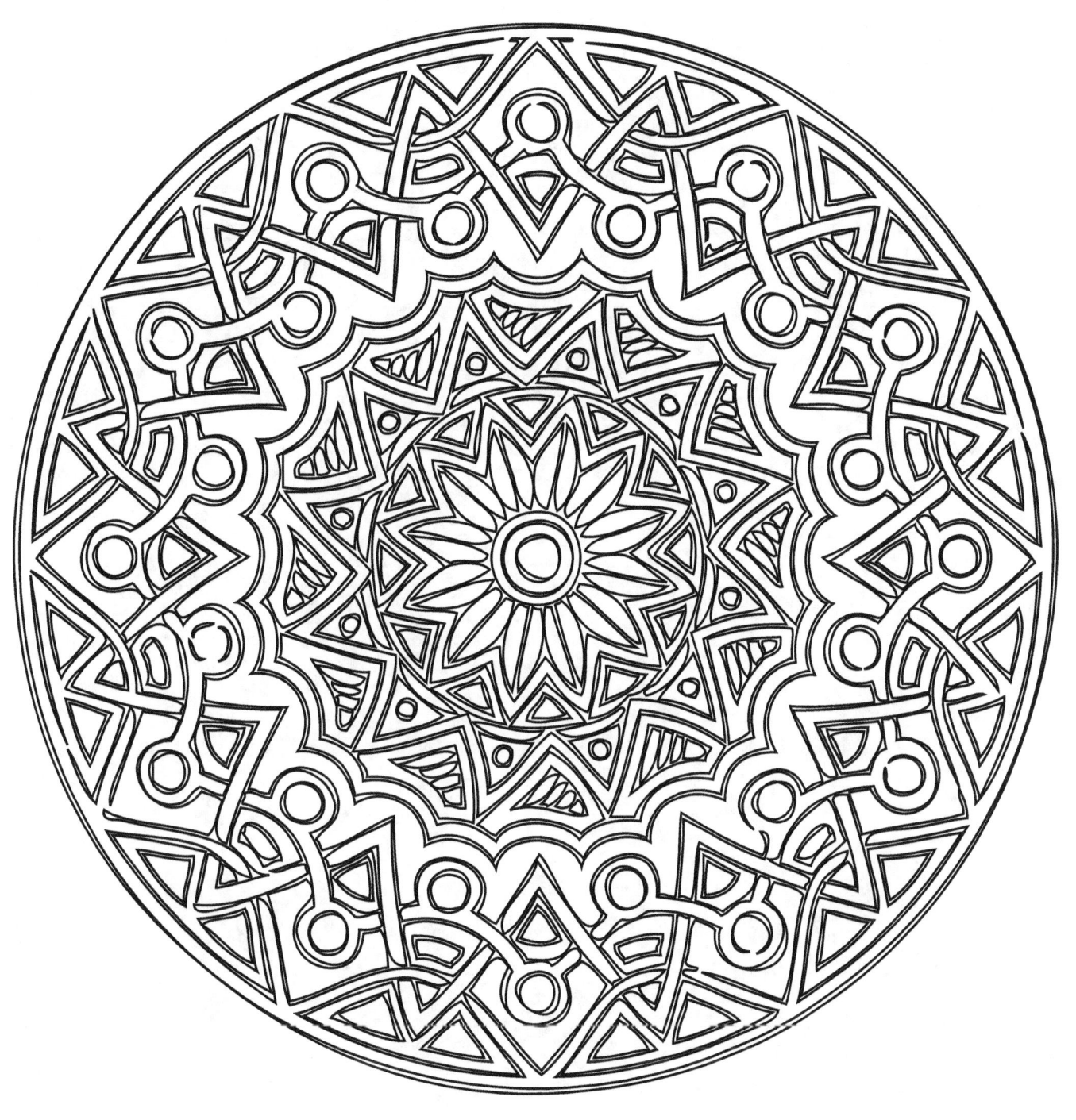

THE LONGER YOU WAIT FOR THE FUTURE,
THE SHORTER IT WILL BE.,
- LOESJE

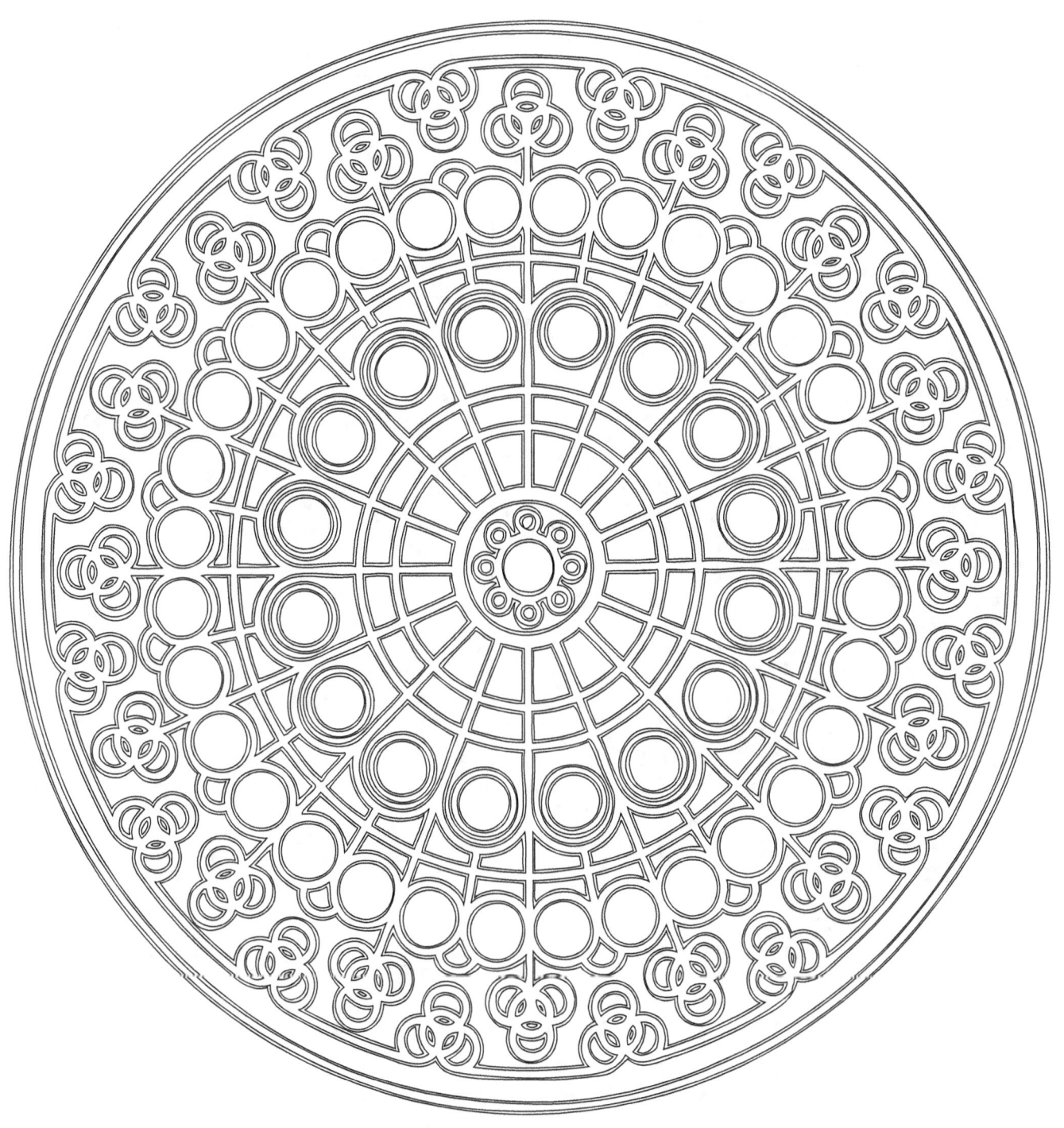

BE SO GOOD, THEY CAN'T IGNORE YOU
- STEVE MARTIN

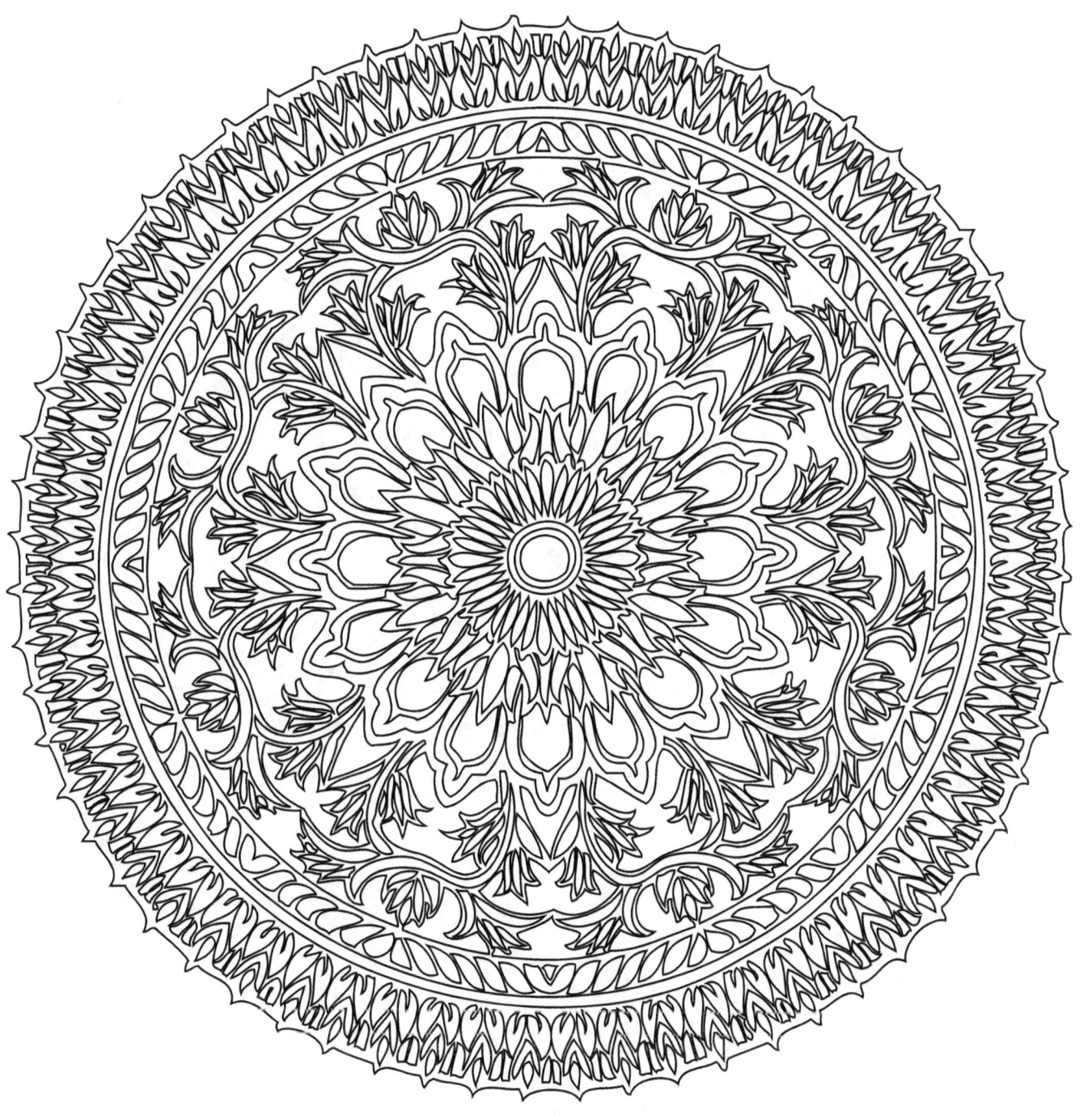

OPPORTUNITIES DON'T JUST HAPPEN,
YOU CREATE THEM.
- CHRIS GOSSER

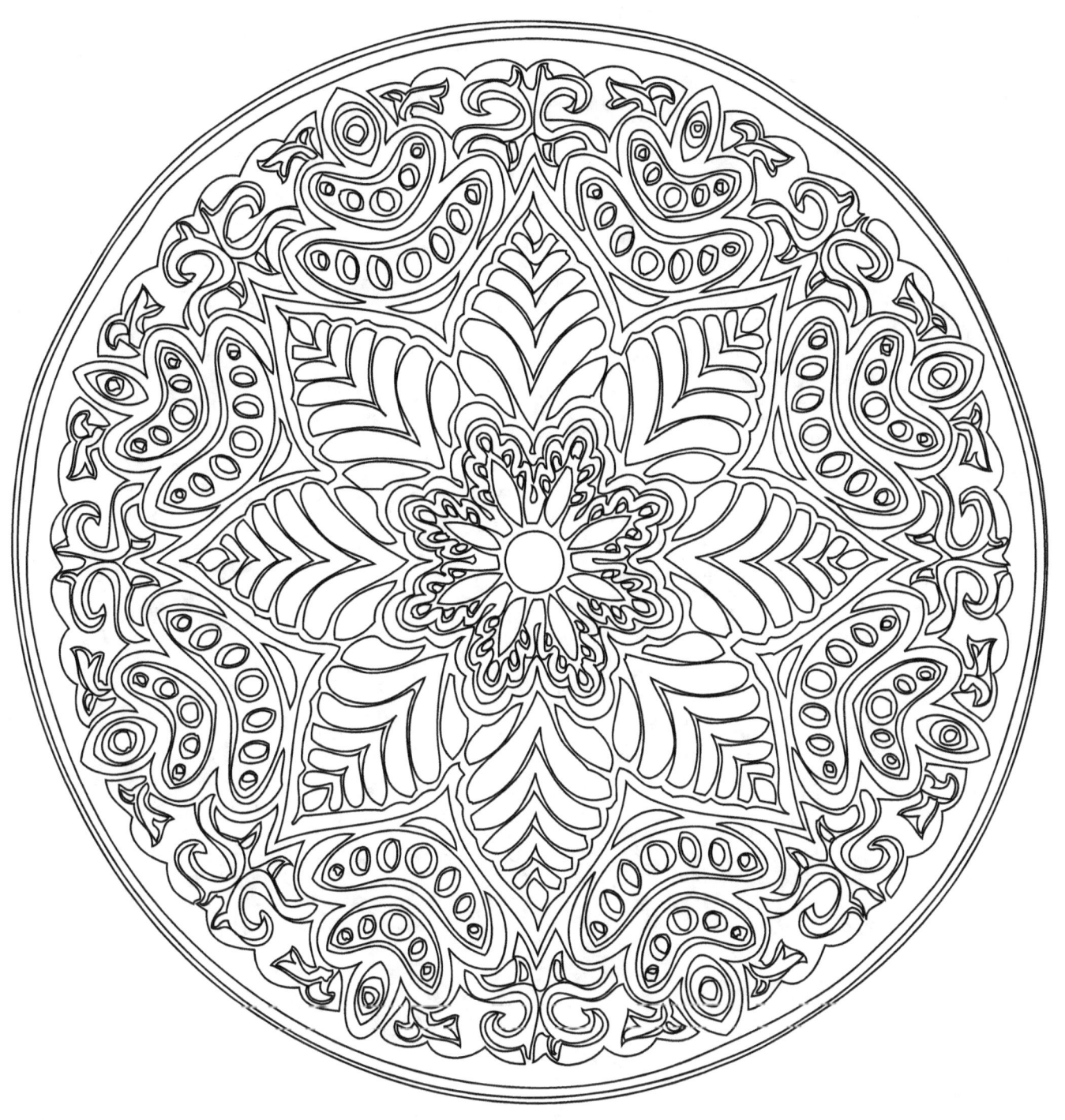

YOU MAY BE DISAPPOINTED IF YOU FAIL,
BUT YOU ARE DOOMED IF YOU DON'T TRY.
- BEVERLY SILLS

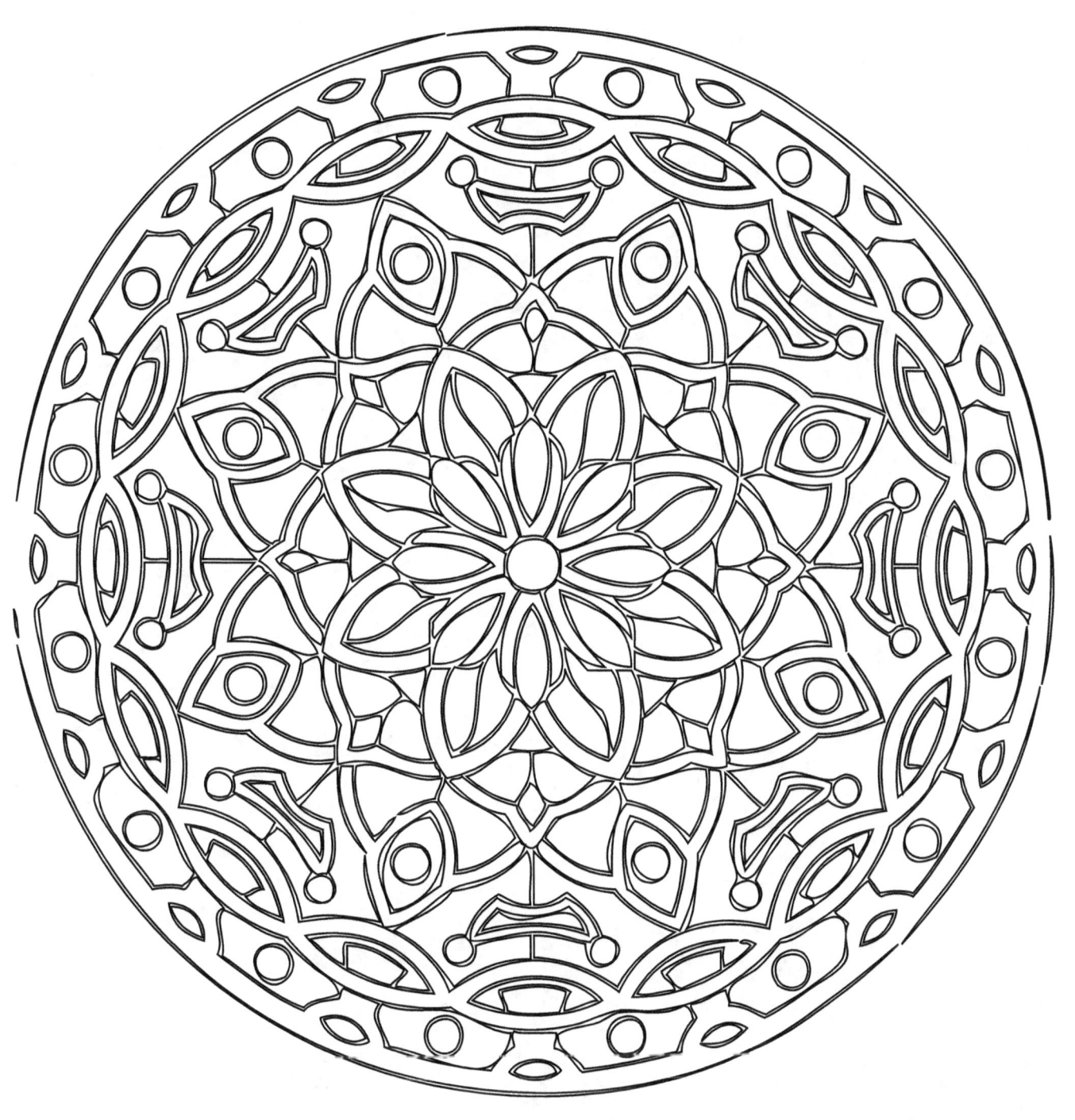

LIFE IS *WHAT* HAPPENS TO YOU *WHILE*
YOU'RE BUSY MAKING OTHER PLANS.
- JOHN LENNON

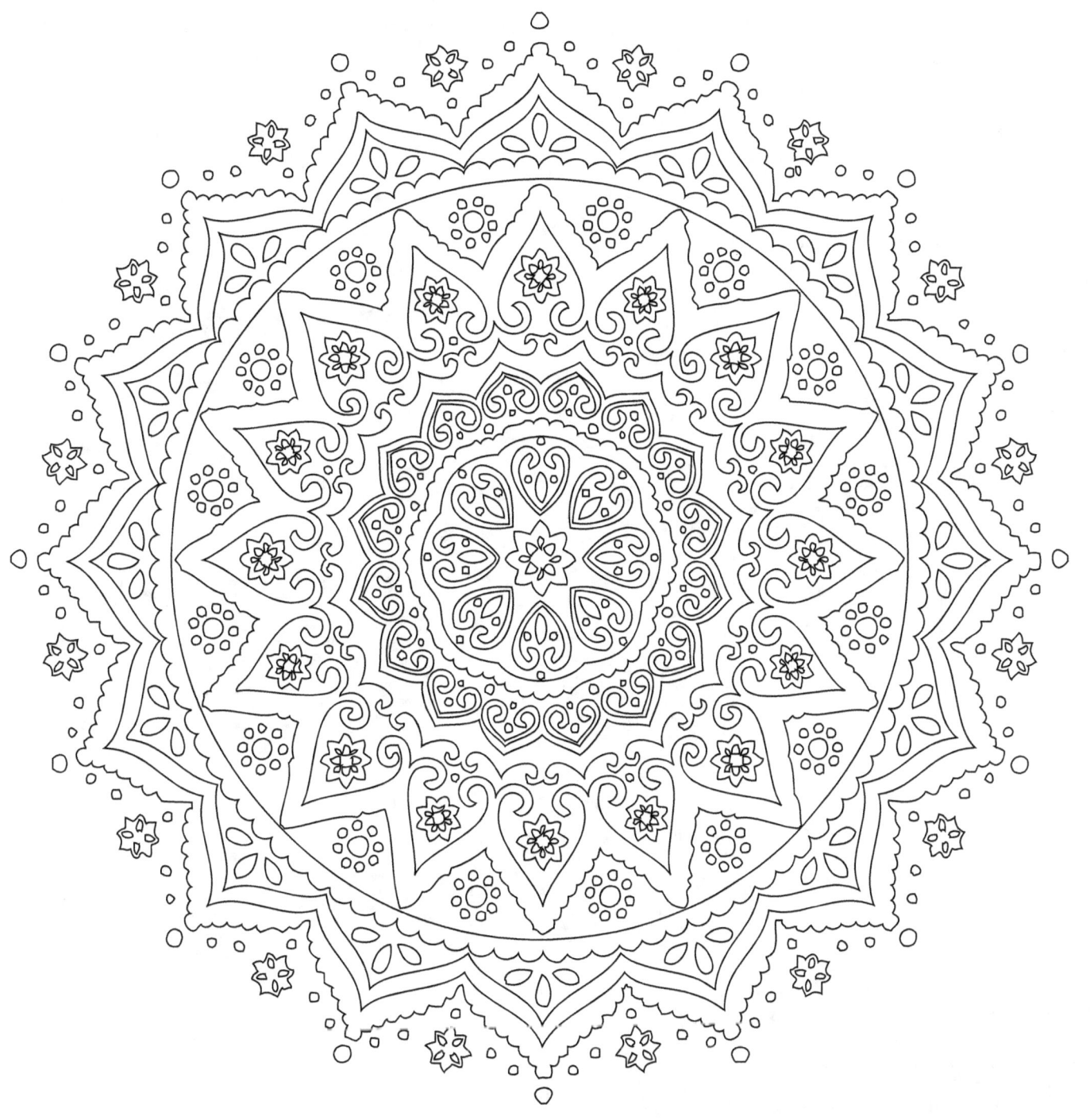

HARD WORK BEATS TALENT WHEN TALENT
DOESN'T WORK HARD.
- TIM NOTKE

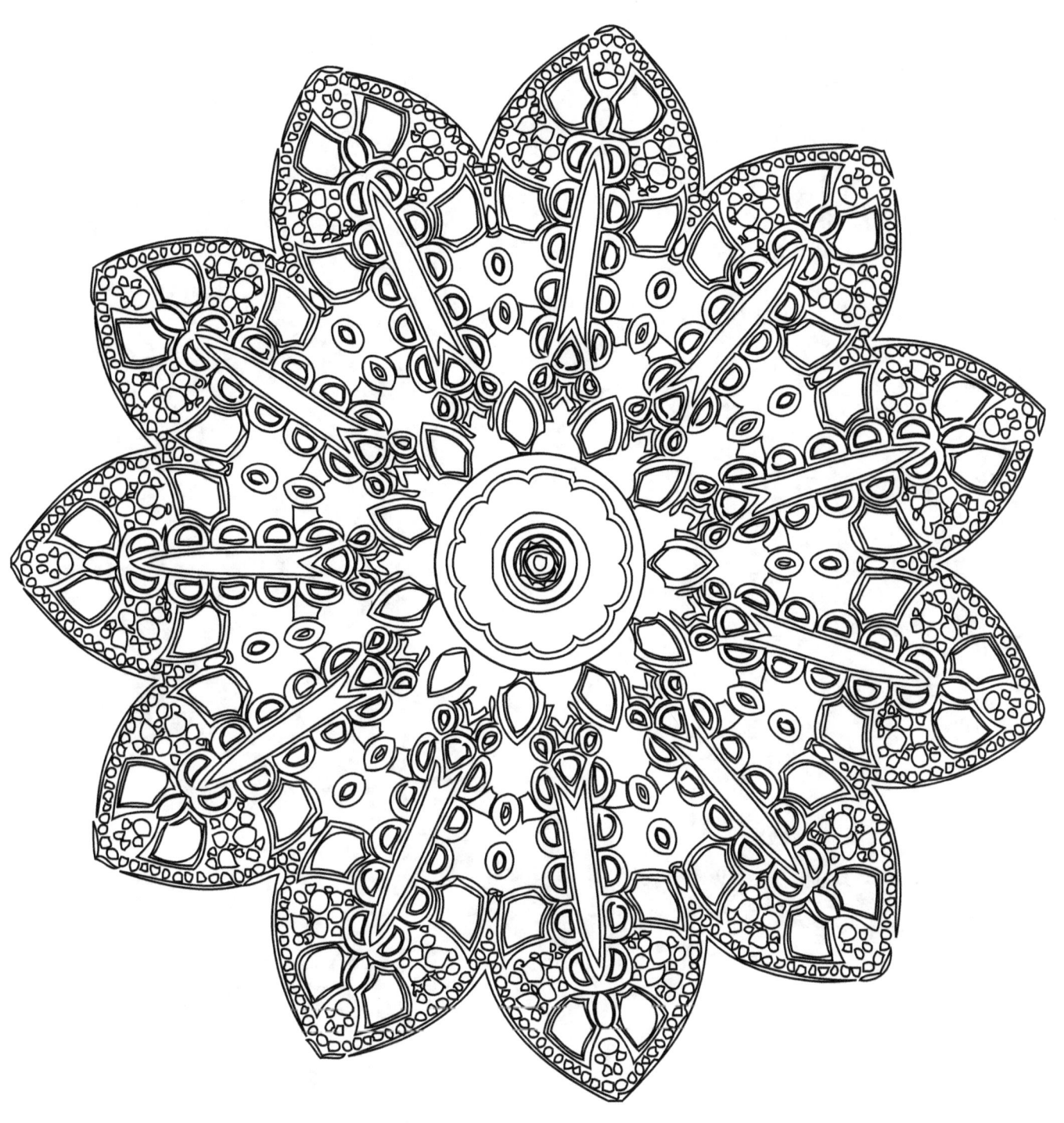

FOCUS. OTHERWISE YOU WILL FIND LIFE
BECOMES A BLUR.
- JPP

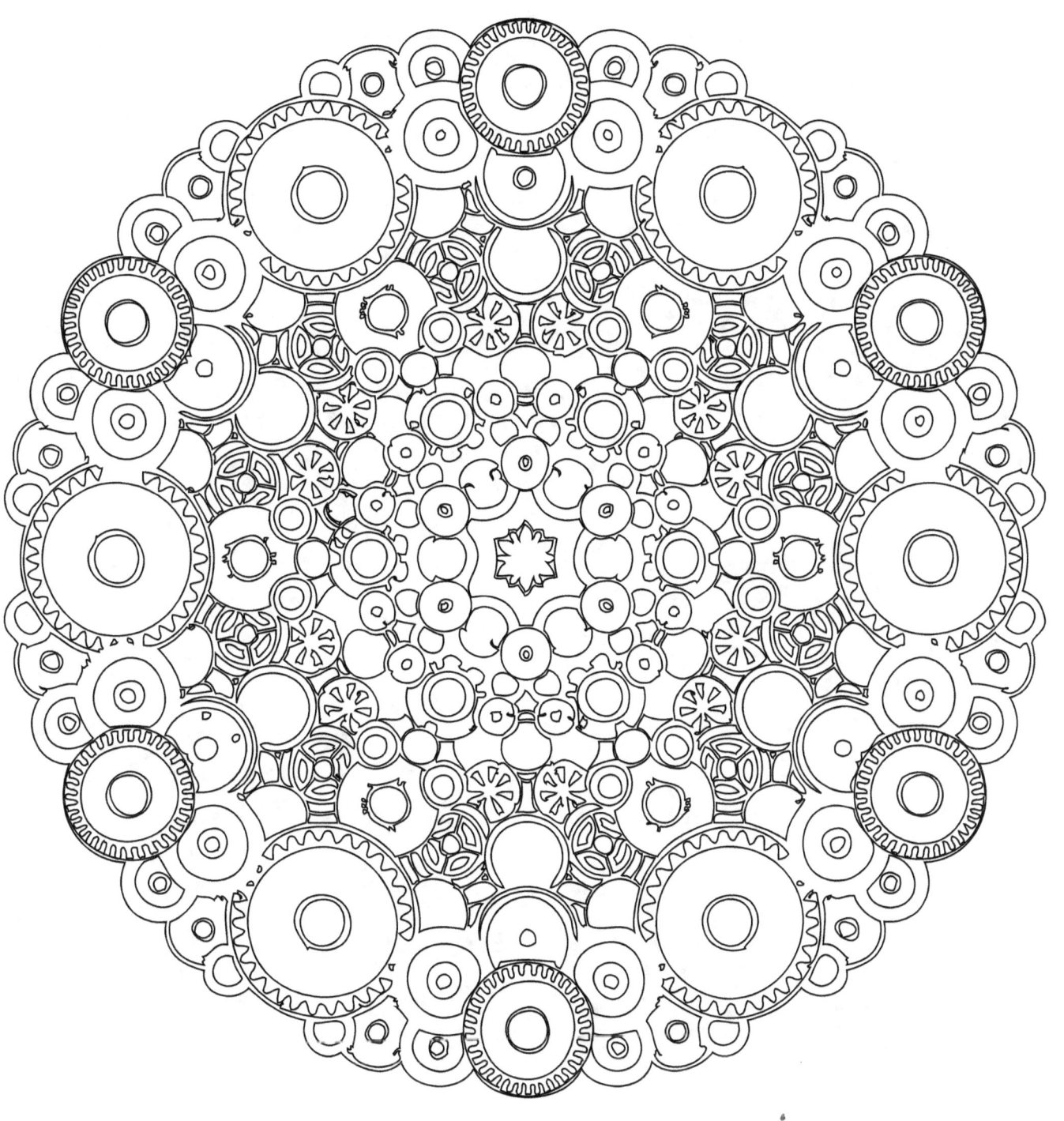

THE ONLY WAY TO DO GREAT WORK IS
TO LOVE WHAT YOU DO.
- STEVE JOBS

www.ingramcontent.com/pod-product-compliance
Lightning Source LLC
Chambersburg PA
CBHW080826180526
45168CB00006B/2583